Secularization and the University

SECULARIZATION AND THE UNIVERSITY

Harry E. Smith

Foreword by Harvey Cox

JOHN KNOX PRESS
Richmond, Virginia

Library of Congress Catalog Card Number: 68-25015

© M. E. Bratcher 1968

Printed in the United States of America

24-0715

This book is dedicated to the memory of my father,

WILLIAM ARTHUR "BLOCK" SMITH,

who taught me how to love and to criticize
the university.

263651

Acknowledgments

Just when the traditional theological efforts to understand and to analyze higher education appeared to have reached an impasse in the late 1950's, a Danforth Campus Ministry Grant and a Kent Fellowship made possible a sojourn away from the campus ministry for doctoral study and afforded me an opportunity to search for a more relevant theological standpoint from which to survey the University. Through Professors John Godsey and Carl Michalson of Drew University, I was introduced to the thought of Dietrich Bonhoeffer and Friedrich Gogarten and their concern for "secularization."

Subsequent efforts at re-viewing the perennial relation of faith and learning, of religion and higher education, were enriched by the warnings and questions of Dean Stanley R. Hopper and Professor Will Herberg of Drew, as well as Professors Waldo Beach and William Poteat of Duke, Professor J. Edward Dirks of Yale, Professors Arnold Nash and Samuel S. Hill of the University of North Carolina, and Professor Charles McCoy of the Pacific School of Religion. All are to be thanked for their criticisms and concern, but none should be reckoned accountable for or even in agreement with what follows.

I am indebted as well to many colleagues in the campus ministry and to the faculty and students at the university I know best for teaching me much of what I know about higher education, and for calling into question many of the facile assumptions with which I once approached and neatly resolved the issues with which this book is concerned.

Most of all, I owe to my wife, Anne, and to our three children, Leslie, Malcolm, and Laurie, an unpayable debt for their patience during the process of getting down on paper these reflections on the questions which haunt anyone trying to relate the biblical faith to the life of a secular university today.

HARRY E. SMITH
Chapel Hill, North Carolina

Foreword

In recent years a staggering number of books has appeared whose titles include the word "secular" or the word "secularization." What was once a forbidden thought for Christian thinkers, the "secular," has now become almost a rallying cry. Still, most readers approach the whole field of "secular theology" or a "theology of the secular" with understandable apprehensiveness. Despite much discussion the word "secularization" retains vague and fuzzy overtones. Despite its usefulness as a "hinge category," opening a door for discussion among theologians, sociologists, literary critics, historians, and others, the word often seems slippery and imprecise. Some readers suspect it may be too general a term, a cloak which covers a multitude of more singular trends.

Harry Smith has done both the current discussion and the term "secularization" a good deed. At the very beginning of this book he comes clean about his theological presuppositions and his definitional starting point. He takes the theological contributions of Friedrich Gogarten and Dietrich Bonhoeffer and uses them to spell out precisely what he means when he uses the word "secular." In doing so he provides the reader, almost incidentally, with a very accurate and precise statement of the theology of these two influential thinkers, as fair a rehearsal of their perspectives as one will find anywhere in such short compass. He also gives us something we can agree with or disagree with, a clear theological option devoid of the fog and drizzle which often beclouds such writing.

If Smith has not introduced much critical commentary on Bonhoeffer or Gogarten this is largely because his book is intended as an application of their thinking on secularization to one specific area of human activity, "higher education." This confrontation of theology and the American university is the heart of the book, and a vibrant, pulsating heart it is. Smith's pages on the history of the university in America reveal that he not only knows it but loves it. He is both a churchman and a man of the university. He appreciates both the church's invaluable contribution to higher education in America and elsewhere, and the very good reasons why the university had to break away from ecclesiastical tutelage. Only a person with these two loyalties and their respective competencies could have written this book.

The version of Christian faith Smith relies on here is really a contemporary restatement of the classical Protestant doctrine of justification by faith. God liberates man from his compulsive search for an ultimate and all-inclusive meaning. He is freed to live with partial truths and limited perspectives, and is reminded at the same time that they are partial and limited so he is not tempted to escalate his own truth into a total system. As Smith says, Christian faith maintains "the true secularity of history by insisting that any unity or wholeness it has comes from God, and that no human effort to supply a unified philosophy of history can provide an ultimately satisfying interpretation of its meaning."

This is certainly acceptable as far as it goes. A question does remain, however, in the mind of Smith and of other celebrants of the secular, as to whether this sort of *theologia negativa* is really the last word the church has for the world. Does the gospel merely save us from idolatry? Or does it also offer us a vision, however provisional, of the Kingdom of God? The question left unresolved by this book, as it has been left unresolved by most theologians today, is how the church can proclaim the positive side of the gospel without lapsing again into closed world-views and static systems. If, as Bonhoeffer insisted and Smith reminds us, secularization is "a clearing of the decks for the God of the Bible," what happens after the decks are cleared?

In this connection it may strike some readers as strange that Smith uses as his principal theological resources two continental theologians. Is there nothing in American theology which could have provided this basis? The answer is that in a society such as ours, which despite its official separation of church and state has retained a persistent residue of Christendom thinking, the corrective of the Europeans is needed. They know better than we do that God is not world, church is not society, faith is not information. They help us in the deck-clearing process. In the next stage, however, they may not be as useful. How will the questions of this next stage present themselves?

As this preface is being written, the campuses of America are seething with discussions about the alleged immorality of the university's "openness" and expansive appreciation for truth from all quarters. Students picket military recruiters, boycott the classes of professors engaged in classified research, and blockade representatives of weapons producers. All this raises once again the question of whether mere openness and a *Wertfrei* posture suffice for the university today.

For some time now we have emphasized the need for "excellence" in the university. But what about the ancient notion of the university as the "Republic of Virtue"? Is it time to explore again that idea? If it is, what are the grounds of virtue? How can it be taught and lived? Are we not once again face to face with some very difficult theological issues?

I think we are. But I do not think in the next phase of the ever-changing encounter between the church and the university, the community of faith and the house of intellect, we can ever leave behind the invaluable lessons taught us by the theologians of the secular. Harry Smith has masterfully applied these lessons to the church's relationship to the university. He thus helps save us from relapsing into a pre-Bonhoeffer hankering for the days when theology was queen and religion "unified" all knowledge. That time is now gone, and we must digest that fact before the next stage is possible. Otherwise the university's new openness to questions of "virtue" and "commitment" could lead us backward rather than forward. Smith's final chapters suggest that he is ready to move forward and to do so utilizing the hard-won insights so carefully and readably presented in this book.

For those who want to know what the best contemporary theology contributes to the best current thinking about the university this book is therefore indispensable. However, after reading it, especially its emphasis on change and movement toward the future, there will remain no possibility except to move on.

HARVEY COX
Harvard University

Contents

Secularization and the University

CHAPTER 1

Introduction

In the ordinary usage of contemporary American Protestantism few terms elicit a more negative response than "secularization." Whether it be in a Sunday sermon attacking "the secular" as materialistic, or a denominational magazine decrying the "tragic triumph of secularism" in the Supreme Court rulings forbidding prescribed prayers in public schools, or a college baccalaurcate address deploring the "secularization" of America's colleges and universities, the term is surrounded by negative, ominous, albeit ambiguous, connotations. Until recently, there were few causes more sure of accord among American churchmen than full-scale opposition to secularization, and there were few areas of public life where this issue was more sharply joined, and therefore widely debated, than in the area of higher education.

Although Roman Catholic theologians have always been able to claim a certain clarity in their understanding of "secularization" as the confiscation of church properties and functions by worldly ("secular") or non-ecclesiastical authorities, or as the relaxation of religious rules in order to permit a "religious" to live outside the cloister in the world,[1] in Protestant circles the term has been variously used to mean removal from denominational or clerical control, loss of a transcendent dimension, hostility to traditional theology, and preoccupation with temporal or material things as opposed to eternal or "spiritual" ones. This ambiguity was abated somewhat in the middle of the nineteenth century when the British humanist George Jacob Holyoake, in reaction against the church of his day, codified the principles of free thought in his "Secularists' Creed" and defined "secularism" for the first time as "a form of opinion relating to the duty of this life founded on considerations purely human, and intended mainly for those who find theology indefinite or inadequate, unreliable or unbelievable."[2]

Recent church history records that it was just such an understanding of "secularism" as "a way of life and meaning of life which takes into consideration only the natural order of things and does not regard God or a realm of spiritual reality as essential for life and thought" which was pondered by the Jerusalem Conference of the International Missionary Council in 1928 and designated an object of Christian evangelization. Yet an attempt was made there to distinguish between the process of secularization for which the Christian faith bears some responsibility and secularism as an attitude of indifference or hostility toward questions of religion and faith.[3]

It may be observed that most Christians continue to look with suspicion upon any factor which contributes to "secularization" and use this term as a designation for any attack upon presuppositions, resistance to ecclesiastical control, or questioning of traditional religious practices. Secularization remains, in popular thought at least, a process of enervation which is contrary and threatening to all that Christianity represents.

It came as something of a shock, therefore, when little more than a decade ago a group of German and Dutch theologians began insisting that the widespread secularism which marks our age is a perverted offshoot of a historical process which is not to be opposed but considered the result of the biblical understanding of the world and man's relation to it. Using such curious phrases as "the abolition of religion," "freedom for the world," "legitimate profanity," "the world come of age," "worldly Christianity," and "holy worldliness"—all in a theological context—these writers suggested a way of viewing the historical-spiritual development since the Renaissance which makes the Christian faith far more responsible for the present cultural situation than most previous interpretations. In developing a "theology of the secular," these writers suggested insights which have pregnant implications for viewing the relation of faith and culture, theology and Western philosophy, and religion and higher education. Regarding secularization not as the greatest threat to Western civilization, "sapping its vitality and menacing its future,"[4] they have been insisting, rather, that secularization is a destiny-fulfilling historical phenomenon which can best be understood theologically.

The context of this discussion can be variously described.

Viewed philosophically, secularization occurs within and is an integral part of that dissolution of a sense of wholeness and orderliness which has characterized Western thought in the last three centuries and suggests the classical problem of the relation of the One and the Many. It entails the loss of any single, fixed frame of reference or overarching world-view and a recognition that there are many different perspectives and standpoints from which reality may be viewed and interpreted. A suspicion of total explanations has also cast doubt upon most traditional, essentialistic definitions and the substantialistic categories of earlier metaphysical systems.

In contrast to the mechanical regularity and assurance of precision and predictability in the preceding era, talk of indeterminacy, discontinuity, and relativity within modern science has necessitated a stance of tentativeness and expectant uncertainty which is much less sure about ultimate order or coherence in the universe. In this sense, modern man has undergone two traumatic uprootings—the one from Christian dogma as an all-embracing metaphysical system, and the other from scientific dogma as an orderly world-view which admits no discontinuities or unforeseen variation.[5]

Mastery over nature and the processes of production in technology has led to the stripping away of any magical, spiritual properties in nature and human life, the disenchantment of the world, and the disappearance of any sense of awe or mystery, or recognition of a dimension of depth in existence. The concern which Gabriel Marcel, Karl Jaspers, Martin Heidegger, and others have expressed about the manipulative attitude of modern man toward life arises from a recognition that nature has been desacralized, but at the same time our inner lives have been impoverished by the abortion of any awareness of transcendence or openness to ultimate meaning in human existence today.

The current exposure of the emptiness of traditional words and existing cultural symbols and the search for new images to communicate meaning together make up but another dimension of the radical change in the consciousness of Western man labeled "secularization." Whether the posture is one of "imaging" in Jungian archetypes from the collective unconscious, or dramatically portraying the absurdity of clichéd conversation, pitching philosophy in a "new key" in terms of symbolic forms, or simply "waiting" in this interim time of spiritual dearth when the old forms of meaning are exposed as hollow and the new forms of meaning have not yet been disclosed, the starting point is the same—recognition that some process has robbed once-powerful images and symbols of their inherent meaning and purpose.

Viewed politically, secularization is closely related to the emergence and acceptance of religious pluralism and the interpretation or enactment of laws protecting the diversity of religious commitments which follows the disestablishment of a particular faith. In the United States this has assumed increasing prominence in efforts to effect a clearer delineation between church and state, and in the mounting protest against any semblance of religious domination. In such a context, where any religious commitment is regarded as "sectarian," the process of secularization is one of "de-religionization," or separation of political and educational structures from the control or traditional practices of any religious group. It is also reflected in the rehabilitation of the concept of the "secular state" among religious leaders and the emergence of self-designated "secular states" in previously "religious" cultures, e.g., India, Indonesia, and Ghana.[6] Roman Catholic leaders are also reemphasizing the Thomist doctrine of "the sovereign independence of the state in its own domain, the temporal order" and insisting that *in a country which is divided in the matter of religious belief,* the state should allow each citizen to practice his religion freely."[7]

Secularization is discussed within educational circles as the fragmentation of knowledge and conflicting claims to absolute truth within various disciplines and departments, the compartmentalization of learning which accompanies increasing specialization, and the heightened diversity within higher education which makes it virtually meaningless today to speak in any substantive way about the "nature of the university" as John Henry Newman did. The same breakdown of any unified metaphysical world-view (if ever there was one) and the multiplicity of truth "standpoints," symbol systems, and models for meaning can be found within the universities, suggesting that the process of secularization in higher education involves not simply the termination of denominational control or the abolition of traditional religious services, but a much more radical reorientation in relation to the nature of truth, the learning process, and the function of education itself.

Within contemporary theology, this discussion takes place among those who are seeking to explore the implications of Friedrich Nietzsche's assertion that "God is dead," viewed no longer as an anti-Christian, but "post-Christian" symbol. A theological analysis of secularization involves not so much a castigation of those external cultural forces which have rendered the name of God so vacuous, as a reappraisal of the relation of faith to the religious and institutional forms it assumes, and a sharp critique of those "religious factors" which have produced the "dishabilitation of the Christian tradition" (Gabriel Vahanian). On the one hand this has led some to attack religion itself as the enemy of faith and to call Christians to authentic existence outside religious institutions.[8] On the other hand, it has produced a score of penetrating analyses of "religion-in-general" (Martin Marty), "operative religion" (Will Herberg), "folk religion" (A. Roy Eckardt), and "religiosity" (Vahanian) which assume that biblical faith not only stands in judgment upon, but can also purify or at least "keep relative," the existing embodiments of religion.

Considered theologically, secularization is the acceptance of fragmentation in theology, as well as in philosophy. If the time for all-embracing metaphysical explanations in philosophy has passed, the time for massive, systematic summae in theology is passing, or at least so it is contended by those theologians today who assiduously avoid systematizing and prefer instead limited, unpretentious exploration of certain biblical themes. This aversion is not simply the work of some external pressures which have undermined confidence in theological system-building, however, but something within the nature of the Christian faith itself as now understood.

The search for meaningful theological language and symbols

is but another aspect of the same discussion, as theologians are becoming increasingly aware that persons today understand themselves in a completely different way from the cultural situation in which most traditional doctrinal formulas were developed. The current preoccupation with religious language arises from the recognition that something has drained the symbolic power from traditional religious images and that a change in man's understanding of himself and his world necessitates a change in his way of talking and thinking about God.

The impact of existential philosophy has heightened interest in explicating the relation between faith and history and the distinction between nature and history, and in exploring the implications of the unique historiography implicit in the Christian faith. In this context the process of secularization is bound up with the shift from viewing history as insignificant beside suprahistorical redemptive acts in medieval thought, to regarding history as the all-important process of self-determination and openness to the future in contemporary existentialism.[9] The question of historiography is variously framed, but in every case it reflects a recognition that man now understands himself historically, hence with a new sense of responsibility not just for studying the past but for shaping the future.

Viewed sociologically, the discussion of secularization is joined with the effort to explain the loss of hegemony by religious leaders and organizations, the disparagement of the popular image of the minister in American culture, and the anti-clericalism which is developing within the churches. From outside its structure, this is reflected in charges of irrelevancy and opportunism directed against the church. From inside it assumes the form of agonizing reappraisals of the churches' need to take seriously the changing structures of American urban life, to reject the clericalism which dominates the institutional church and seeks to exercise control over men's lives in the world, and to provide something more than acquiescence and divine endorsement of prevailing cultural values and practices.

This cursory sketch of the current context for discussion suggests issues far beyond the scope of this book. Yet the great ferment taking place in every area of life today is inextricably related to that process of change in the consciousness of Western man generally labeled "secularization."

Conceived as a prolegomenon to the development of a philosophy of higher education grounded in both the Christian faith and the secular world, this book begins by examining the use of the term "secularization" in the writings of the two contemporary Protestant theologians most influential in its reinterpretation, Friedrich Gogarten and Dietrich Bonhoeffer. After reviewing evidences of secularization in Western thought, it then explores some of the implications of their theological interpretation of secularization for understanding the development of higher education in the United States and for viewing the relation between the Christian faith and secular universities.

CHAPTER 2

The Reinterpretation of Secularization in Contemporary Theology

Although the concept of secularization has been receiving increasing attention in theological circles in the past two decades, it is still largely interpreted as the alienation of man from God and hence a process to be opposed by the church and all men of faith.

Recent efforts to develop a theological reinterpretation of the process of secularization find their roots in and affinity to the biblical way of viewing man's relation to God and to the world, and insist that the terms "secular," "secularity," and "secularization" be rehabilitated from their traditional pejorative use. Although the literature both furthering and refuting this theological effort is voluminous and increasing monthly, the seminal thinkers remain Friedrich Gogarten and Dietrich Bonhoeffer. Acknowledged repeatedly by Ronald Gregor Smith, Daniel Jenkins, J. A. T. Robinson, Denis Munby, Carl Michalson, Harvey Cox, James Pike, William Hamilton, Gibson Winter, Larry Shiner, and Martin Marty—to name but a few of the English and American writers on "secularization"—is an indebtedness to insights first suggested by these two German theologians. Hence, it is with their thought about secularization that we must begin.

SECULARIZATION IN THE THOUGHT OF FRIEDRICH GOGARTEN

"What happens in secularization?" has been a recurrent question throughout the later writings of Friedrich Gogarten. Although treated implicitly in earlier writings, his conviction that the process of secularization is rooted in and sustained by biblical faith was first treated within the framework of Western intellectual history in *Der Mensch zwischen Gott und Welt* (1952), and given explicit theological consideration in *Verhängnis und Hoffnung der Neuzeit: Die Säkularisierung als theologisches Problem* (1953) and *Was ist Christentum?* (1956). Whether discussing the problem of subjectivism in contemporary theology in *The Reality of Faith* or defending Rudolf Bultmann's program of demythologizing in *Demythologizing and History*, Gogarten has been preoccupied with secularization in his postwar works and has discussed it repeatedly in his effort to explain theologically what has happened in Western man's understanding of himself and his world. Nowhere does the "symphonic" nature of his unsystematic theology become clearer than here, as this persistent, haunting theme is introduced in ever new settings. Certainly Gogarten is in the tradition of those who reject any systematic, dogmatic theology and are content, rather, to elaborate various themes. Crucial for Gogarten has been the theme of secularization.[1]

Recognizing that in popular parlance the term originally meant the transfer of properties "from a sacred, God-serving purpose to a worldly, secular use," Gogarten cites the seizure of monasteries at the time of the Reformation as the classic illustration of "secularization." More recently, he notes, the term has been used of the process whereby ideas or knowledge which were originally Christian in appearance and were received by believers from God through revelation are now thought to be accessible to all men by reason, entirely unaided by faith.[2] Sustained by his reason alone, man seems able now to create and shape reality, responsible to himself alone.

Whereas the latter definition of the term has usually provoked great anxiety among churchmen and the frantic demand that the church "put an end to secularization," Gogarten considers this a process arising directly out of the Christian faith, which has produced "changes in the structure of human existence which can never again be canceled."[3] These changes involve far more than the simple usurping of certain ideas by reason from faith, or the materialistic accumulation of wealth which weakened the "cloistered asceticism" of the Middle Ages, or the cutting off of ecclesiastical control in such areas as education, legal systems, and research. Rather, secularization denotes a process in which man's self-understanding is transformed as a direct result of the Christian interpretation of human existence, a process which did not happen just once but has to happen again and again as man seeks to discover who he is in relation to the world.

Any understanding of how this term functions in Gogarten's thought requires a careful examination of the way in which certain constituent concepts—world, self, freedom, and history—have been transformed in their meaning and use because of the Christian faith. Only thus can one determine what Gogarten means when he asserts that "the most remarkable thing which occurs in secularization is that the independence of man in the radical sense he possesses it in the contemporary world can be acquired only through the knowledge and experience made accessible in the Christian faith."[4]

Such conceptual analysis will clarify how the ambiguity in the use of "secularization" is the result of the very change in the use of its constituent concepts. For although the term was used initially in conjunction with particular and self-evident understandings of the world, truth, history, and religious authority, these meanings are no longer self-evident for modern man. This is the basis of the need Gogarten finds to display more fully the present understanding of these terms in a theological setting in order to demonstrate the usefulness of "secularization" as a descriptive category for understanding what has happened in Western thought.

Although such a "contextual study" scarcely does justice to the totality of Gogarten's theological enterprise, neglecting such pivotal themes as his Christology and eschatology, it does reveal a thematic continuity by examining the various settings in which the concept appears.

Man in Relation to God and the World

For the pre-Christian man, the world was thought to be all-embracing and ultimate. "Its eternal order [was] the fundamental problem. The decisive issue for man, therefore, [was] both *that* and *how* he [might] adapt himself and his actions to this order."[5] Understanding himself solely on the basis of this world, man tended to worship the creation rather than the Creator. The elemental spirits who were believed to give order to the world were the guardians of his life.

Gogarten's use of the word "world" here includes both nature, which to the primitive mind was permeated by irrational powers and gods before whom man trembled and offered his worship, and the ordered cosmos of the later Greeks. In both cases, man was enclosed by his world, feeling that all he could do was to try to understand it and subordinate himself to its elements. To be "of the world" was to be in bondage to its mysterious powers. In spite of the Greeks' profound consideration of the cosmos, their enclosed existence could not be overcome by any reflection upon it, Gogarten insists; they remained cosmic beings, belonging to the world.[6]

By proclaiming a God who created the world and governs beyond what seemed holy to the ancients—the cosmos and state—yet one who enters into history in the incarnation, crucifixion, and resurrection of Jesus Christ, the Christian faith dethroned the ruling powers of the world and freed man from the tyranny of the spirits who were thought to permeate everything. It was not these powers, any more than it was the world itself, which the Christian faith opposed. It was bondage to these powers, worship of the elemental spirits of nature as mysterious, divine reality, and hence enclosure by the world against God, which the Christian faith attacked. It was the *status* ascribed by man to the powers of lawfulness and order in the world which gave them a demonic quality.

Since there is no relation of man to God which does not, at the same time, involve a relation to the world, and vice versa, man's freedom for God requires his liberation from bondage to the world. Hence Gogarten is able to make the distinction between those who think of themselves as sons of God and therefore responsible to him, and those who still receive their understanding of who they are from the world and its laws and remain enclosed by them. The latter forfeit their freedom by enslaving themselves to the world, remaining responsible to it. The former have learned that freedom for God means, however, not only freedom from domination by the world but also responsibility for the world, seen now as creation, not worshiped as creator.

Since his freedom is genuine freedom, man is constantly confronted with the necessity for choosing between God and the world. To accept freedom for God is to see the world in its proper perspective, as man's responsibility. But to remain responsible to the world means to forfeit this freedom by placing oneself in bondage to the powers of the world, a world which is regarded either mythically, or as a world whose unity and wholeness man has to provide himself.

> The decisive thing is that modern man is no longer responsible to the world and its power as the classical man and, in a modified way, even the medieval man was. Instead, he has become the one who is responsible *for* his world. . . . faith, by the power of the freedom for God safeguarded by it and accessible in it, opens to man at one and the same time freedom for himself and independence toward the world. . . . The test of this independence as well as its character is expressed in the fact that man no longer is responsible *before* the world and its law, as he was in pre-Christian times. He is rather responsible *for* the world and its law. In virtue of that, the religious power of the world and its law is ended.[7]

The development of science is one result of freedom from the religious attitude toward the world, according to Gogarten, for it is a part of man's effort to accept responsibility for the world by investigating and understanding its orderly functioning. He uses the German word *Wahrnehmung*, which means "perception and observation," as well as "maintenance and protection" of the world.[8]

In this context, secularization is conceived as the recognition and maintenance of the worldliness of the world, seeing "that in every case and in every respect and in everything that belongs to it, the world is and remains what it is—just world."[9] The many gods and demons which were earlier believed to permeate and dominate the world are deprived of their power, and the world is seen as only world, that is, a world which is secular. After the "de-demonization" of the world, man needs no longer to hold the world and its power in reverence and awe but is free from a world which has had its sacral power extorted from it. It is this use of "secularization" which Gerhard Ebeling has in mind when he asserts that "radical Christian faith contains the seed which de-divinizes the world and makes it truly the world."

> . . . faith makes the world what it truly is, the creation of God. It rids the world of demons and myths, and lets it again be what God wills it to be. Because faith frees us from the world, it frees us for the world. Because it does not live on the world, it makes it possible for us to live for the world. Because it puts an end to the misuse of the world, it opens the way to the right use of the world. Because it breaks the domination of the world, it gives domination over it and responsibility for it. And because it drives out the liking and the misliking of the world, it creates room for pure joy in the world.[10]

This process is responsible for the independence which man feels in relation to the world and is reflected in his new self-understanding.

In thus depicting secularization as the "worldlilization" or "de-idolization" of the world, Gogarten uses the model of Creator and creation to emphasize that man has a different relationship to the world because of the biblical belief that the world is not self-generating. It is the result, rather, of the creative activity of an absolute Creator, and man as creature is related to his Creator in a way quite different from his relation to the rest of creation. Today we think of the world therefore no longer as "divine," "eternal," "sacred," "preestablished," "fateful," but regard it as "derived," "created," "contingent," "dependent," in short, as "just world." As creation, the world is considered dependent upon its Creator in a way he is not dependent upon it; as the responsibility of man in a way man is not responsible to it; as that which is to be examined, controlled, and used by man, rather than that which controls and uses him.

Man in Relation to Himself

If man's understanding of his relation to the world stems from his recognition of God as creator and himself as creature, his self-understanding derives from his recognition of God as father and himself as son. The notion of man's sonship receives repeated emphasis by Gogarten, since it provides an image which holds together man's independence with his creatureliness. Sonship means not only that man knows himself as he is known, as one who receives his being "from the Father," not from the world or from himself; it also means receiving his "filial freedom" or "responsible personhood" from his Father. Thus Gogarten again emphasizes that man's openness to God determines his relationship to the world, for by accepting the implications of his sonship, man becomes aware that he is an heir and thus responsible for his inheritance, the world.

Administration of this world as his inheritance involves both a recognition of its source, and thus a sense of responsibility to the One who bequeaths it, and an acceptance of the responsibility entrusted to man with the inheritance to preserve and safeguard an awareness of the One who gave it to him. To deny either of these by claiming the world is man's creation or by cutting himself off from God as autonomous is to forfeit his filial freedom and any understanding of himself as son. It is not simply to lose some *thing* like power, control, or authority over the world. Rather, it is to forfeit *oneself*, to misuse sonship and return to the pious awe and enslaving anxiety which are marks of bondage to the elemental spirits or laws of the world. ". . . by forfeiting his sonship the son also forfeits his inheritance," for he can no longer "be responsible *for* that on which he relies with his whole life, for he has become responsible *to* it."[11]

Because man remains in submission to the powers of the world and fails to acknowledge his sonship and thus forfeits his true selfhood, the promise of salvation in the Christian faith is the restoration of sonship. For here is an awakened awareness of God's creatorhood in relation to the world and fatherhood in relation to man made visible in the paradigmatic sonship and lordship of Jesus Christ. It is acceptance of freedom from the Father and freedom in relation to the world which enables one to live in maturity and independence. Before this was made possible in faith, man was in the period of minority and subjection to guardianship, a relationship of dependence upon the ordering "elements" and laws of the world. With the offer of restored sonship made possible in Jesus Christ, the Christian faith has initiated the time of mature sonship.

In this context, secularization is viewed positively as the development of self-understanding which results from man's liberation from the enclosing powers and structures of the world, his acceptance from God of his status as free son and responsible heir, and the independence which goes with this. This is the development of the "ethos of maturity."[12] It may lead, however, to the loss of personhood if this twofold understanding of selfhood as "God-derived" and "world-responsible" is forgotten or denied, or if either the obligation of the son or the responsibility of the heir is not accepted.

In his description of secularization as the development of a new self-understanding by modern man, Gogarten uses the model of sonship to illumine the relationship of man to God and the world. In contrast to the notion that man understands himself solely in terms of nature, or other persons, or out of himself, faith in God as father opens up the possibility for man to understand himself not in natural, substantialistic, or generic terms but through the dynamic, personal, and historic model of sonship. Such a figure calls to mind not only the derivedness of selfhood, but also the independence which a son enjoys from his father when he comes of age and the responsibility thrust upon him as an heir when he is trusted and charged with the administration of the inheritance. To be an heir involves not only responsibility for the future administration of the inheritance, but also responsibility to the one bequeathing it. Although sonship can never be obliterated—it is a given, permanent relationship—it can be ignored or forfeited. Hence with this image Gogarten emphasizes the responsibility which is part of our humanness, and at the same time, the freedom which each person has to be disobedient by forfeiting his freedom and thereby his true selfhood.

Human Freedom and Responsibility

Just as sonship involves man's relation both to God and to the world, Gogarten's understanding of human freedom contains the same twofold nature, i.e., freedom for God, and freedom from the world. This duality is described in various ways. At one point it is described as the *freedom for God* in which man receives his sonship from God completely apart from any effort or reasoning on his part, and *freedom for works* in which he acts responsibly in the world. Included in this latter freedom are the autonomous decisions of the human reason, and the establishment and maintenance of law and order in the world.

This is the same distinction which Martin Luther made between justification by faith and works righteousness, reiterating the Pauline distinction between what God does for man through grace which involves his salvation, and what man does with his works because of his responsibility for the world. When this distinction is not maintained, man seeks to save himself by his works, or the law is made a means to salvation as he seeks to do for himself what God has already done for him.

Elsewhere this same distinction is described as the tension between faith and reason. ". . . freedom from the law means that the knowledge of the law and the decision about the works that the law demands are surrendered by faith to the reason as its responsibility."[13] Insisting upon the maintenance of this distinction, Gogarten points out that whereas the law was the realm over against which Paul placed the gospel, in our time of subjectivism not the law but rational responsibility for the world has become all-important, exercising dominion over modern man. It is in his self-sufficient rationalism, not his legalism, that man withholds himself from God.

Thus the distinction between grace and law in Pauline thought and justification by faith and works righteousness in Lutheran thought demands today recognition of the distinction between the divine reality of salvation in faith and the human acceptance of responsibility for the world through the use of reason. Where this distinction is maintained, faith encourages submission to the law, good works, and autonomous exercise of the reason, for these are part of the free life of man in the world, his "ethical maturity." But should they seek to do more, to achieve eternal good or provide ultimate meaning, they come into conflict with faith.

In whatever form this twofold tension is described by Gogarten, whether between faith and reason, freedom of faith and freedom for works, or the law of faith and the law of works, or the divine reality of salvation and human works of the law— all are distinctions which can be made only in the light of faith. Yet all are also distinctions which contribute to the furtherance of secularization. For by limiting the realm in which faith operates to man's salvation and hence repudiating the church's claim to sovereignty over the areas of the world, a *derived* autonomy is granted to man's existence in the world and the orders of life there, a moral self-determination in which man is responsible now for himself. The Apostle Paul began this process in his belabored distinction between gospel and law, but, according to Gogarten, Luther contributed most to it by reasserting this dialectical relationship after it had become blurred in medieval times by the papal claims to spiritual-political worldly power. Luther made possible not only a new understanding of faith as freedom for God, apart from works, but also a new freedom for science and reason by liberating the world and its laws from religious worship and ecclesiastical control and by insisting upon complete freedom of research and instruction in the natural sciences.

Unfortunately, subsequent theological thought, notably the Protestant scholasticism of the next two centuries, either ignored the distinction which Luther had made so vivid or turned his teaching on the two realms into the static spatial distinction between church and state. As a result, instead of recognizing that faith which has come of age "delivered the world as God's creation over to man's reason,"[14] the church considered itself threatened by the autonomous development of reason within the sciences and responded by defensively opposing its findings and by turning the Christian faith into a competing rational world-view.[15]

On the other hand, during the Enlightenment, human reason was accorded such reverence that there was little or no need for faith. Hence the essential polar tension which Luther envisioned was resolved. Without faith to recognize and maintain this distinction, reason began to claim justifying power and to seek to accomplish what only faith can provide, i.e., ultimate meaning and salvation for man.

Thus in the ensuing absence or weakening of faith, a "post-Christian subjectivism" arose, which, according to Gogarten, has enslaved modern man every bit as much as the mysterious and fateful "elements" enslaved primitive man, the law enslaved pre-Christian man, and good works and indulgences enslaved medieval man. As the world-view created by science, subjectivism no longer recognizes

> that man's independence has its source in the creatureliness of man and the world. Independence is now founded upon the prerogative of man . . . on the nature of man himself. Hence, the creaturely man has become a being who can understand himself as man only on the basis of the claim that he is the source of meaning for all being.[16]

In this setting, secularization which arises from faith's recognition of the distinction between God's saving work as creator and father and man's response as heir and son is perverted when either side of this polarity is overlooked, when the church denies man's independence and reason's autonomy and seeks to control all areas of life, reducing the Christian faith to a worldview, or when modern man denies God's fatherhood and the world's derivedness and seeks to become the one "upon whom all being in its way of being and in its truth is based" (Heidegger).

Though inherent in the New Testament understanding of faith, this kind of distinction did not actually come to full expression for fifteen centuries, according to Gogarten, because medieval thought had not liberated itself from classical Greek thought, and human freedom could not be conceived apart from the mediation of religious institutions.

Yet insofar as this distinction led to the autonomy of reason and its independence from domination by scholastic metaphysics and to the freedom of the sciences to explore the natural world apart from the constrictions of substantialistic thought or ecclesiastical control, this process of secularization had the practical effect of destroying the unity of medieval metaphysics and of disengaging first the natural sciences and then other areas of life from the domination of the church. If faith turns over to man's reason the responsibility for understanding the world and dealing responsibly with it, and at the same time makes clear that it can have no justifying power but is simply the way one expresses his maturity as a son before God, then of necessity it instigates a process which threatens the status of theology as queen of the sciences. It also questions the substantialistic order of the medieval world-view, the prevailing conception of natural law, and the authority of the church in such realms as law, politics, education, and art.

> . . . secularization has its beginning in the Christian faith itself. Because faith makes this distinction (between the divine reality of salvation and the works of the law), it guards the works in their earthly-worldly meaning and lets them be an affair of the world, of the *saeculum* surrendered to man's reason. This secularization concerns not only this or that particular action, but in accord with the Christian belief that "all is permitted," all which is turned over to man in the world. Further, this secularization is not a thing of man's inclination. Rather because faith has to make the distinction which is its highest concern in order to remain pure faith, this secularization must happen. And where it has once happened and is halted in the best interests of faith, there one acts against faith. Then faith is no longer that faith by which alone man is justified without the works of the law. Secularization is, therefore, closely connected with that faith which alone justifies man.[17]

Gogarten uses the term "secularization" in this context to designate the inevitable effects of the acceptance of the doctrine of justification by faith, with its sharp distinction between the divine work of salvation and human responsibility for good works in the world. Viewed from one way, this is a process of delimiting faith to the realm of saving wholeness and unity by recognizing that historic faith cannot function as a rational, comprehensive world-view, or as eternal, abstract truths, without becoming perverted into an ideology. This process divested the church of its externally imposed authority in such areas as scientific research and political theory. Viewed from the other side, it is a process of freeing man from the burden of creating or finding ultimate meaning and wholeness for himself, clarifying his status and protecting the autonomy of reason, and liberating the world and its laws from religious worship and ecclesiastical control. Out of his strong Lutheran background, Gogarten draws the conclusion that if faith in God alone provides man's ultimate meaning, then man is freed to participate in the world, to perfect and observe its laws, and to use his autonomous reason, unburdened by the awesome responsibility of earning his own salvation.

The Historicity of Human Existence

Man's freedom from domination by the elemental spirits of nature and responsibility for the forms of the world make possible a new understanding of human existence as historical. Gogarten describes the view of history held by the post-Socratic Greeks in their search for stability in the world. "For them the actual reality of the world consisted not in its changing, not, that is to say, in its history, but in its unalterable being."[18] Insofar as the historical was the transitory, it was not given serious consideration.

In the medieval historical view, the emphasis was upon a trans-temporal plan which is being disclosed in human life; hence what happens in the world was basically only waiting and preparation for divine works of redemption. But such an interpretation ascribed "no historical significance to precisely that which we regard as the actual historical process, namely the vital personal experiences of particular individuals in their particular characters and responsibilities."[19] Thus the Christian understanding of human existence as responsibility for the world was submerged beneath a metaphysic which emphasized transcendent history and saw all world happenings against a suprahistorical background.

The breaking up of the medieval theology of history occurred with the development of the historical thinking which began to consider the world as something to be observed and given a form and order. As the natural sciences began to observe the cosmos as a "causally conducted continuity of events" and nature had its secrets wrested from it, the notion of historically transcendent occurrences of divine redemption became increasingly untenable, and instead of striving to adapt himself to an unalterable preestablished order, man felt a desire to take part in history, to shape and direct it.

To say that the world is historical means for Gogarten that modern man perceives it as his own, "not that he created it, but that it receives its definite historical form more and more from him."[20] The constituent motives of history are that man becomes responsible for his life and conduct and the form of his world and does not simply accept these as predetermined or supernaturally controlled, and that he inquires after the meaning of the whole of human life.

The twofold understanding of wholeness which the Christian faith provides—on the basis of divine activity perceived in faith and on the basis of human rationality—leads to a twofold viewing of history. On the one hand are divine events, acts of redemption for which God is responsible and which are known only in faith. On the other hand are human, earthly events for which man is responsible. The latter, though constantly under the demand for wholeness, neither realize this wholeness nor provide man's ultimate salvation. By making and insisting upon the maintenance of this distinction, faith is able to keep earthly history in its own realm, thus preserving the truly historical character of human events in the world.

To say that man is a historical being means, therefore, that he recognizes the distinction between the divine saving work and human decision, and accepts responsibility for earthly history. In this sense he is no longer a cosmic being, enclosed by the world, nor a mythical being, enslaved by the mysterious elemental spirits, but he is now a historical being. He does not belong to the world in the earlier sense, but, rather, the world belongs to him.

To say that man is historical also means that he is no longer bound by static metaphysical categories which distinguish between nature and supernature, the cosmos and transcendent world, revealed and natural law, and which consider real only what is, was, and has always been valid in all circumstances. What is real for modern man is "what is yet to be, what will come into being through him,"[21] for the world is seen as "a becoming" which does not occur without the help, will, and efforts of man. The hierarchically-ordered metaphysical concepts of medieval theology have broken down, Gogarten repeatedly asserts, because of the responsibility which man now accepts for the world, his openness to the future, and his relationship to God, which is no longer conceived in substantialistic terms. In this sense, instead of clinging to fixed structures and defending the facticity of past events, he accepts in questioning ignorance the obscurity of the future.

Insofar as man knows himself as a temporal, historical person who comes to self-understanding in the ever new decisions which shape his existence, responsibility and historicity are virtually synonymous in Gogarten's thought. Since he uses the term "secularization" to refer to the acceptance of man's freedom from the world and his mastery over it which stem from a Christian understanding of mature sonship, the radical historicization of human existence through Christian faith and the secularization of the world belong together. Secularization in this context is the substitution of the historical world for the mythical one. It is "historification," i.e., recognition of the historical nature of human existence, which corresponds to man's acceptance of this as his world for which he bears responsibility.

Thus modern man no longer conceives of his history as natural fate or predetermined destiny. Understanding himself as responsible for the world, he likewise assumes that he has responsibility for the decisions which shape what is to come. Hence, man's emerging historical consciousness is an awareness that, as a historical agent who is not simply acted upon, he must encounter what is past as a present reality if he is to act decisively in determining his future.

Secularization recognizes and maintains the distinction between divine history and human history by insisting that worldly events are truly historical, that is, man's responsibility. Where this distinction is not maintained and human history claims to satisfy the demand for ultimate wholeness and meaning, or divine history is interpreted in a way which denies human freedom and robs man of responsibility for the world, then secularization has given way to "secularism," whether in a Christian or non-Christian form.

Secularization and Secularism

In each of the contexts in which the concept of secularization has been examined, it has been described as a process originally made possible by the Christian faith. But there have also been hints throughout that when one denies this connection or ignores the necessary dialectical tension which man's relation to God and world presupposes, secularization deteriorates into an "erroneous secularization," or "secularism." In the latter instance, man carries forward the insights provided by faith without acknowledging their source or recognizing their relativity. Because the clear picture of wholeness which man desires is not to be attained through his own efforts but comes only from God, he begins to ascribe an absolute status to his relative meanings and limited reason or to try to silence all questions concerning the wholeness of the world by a pretended omniscience.

The first kind of secularization is "that which remains within the secular, allowing the world to be 'only' world, recognizing not only the limits of reason which considers the idea of the *whole* as the highest achievement of thought, but at the same time, never trying to answer or reach beyond a questioning ignorance."[22] Involved here is a humility which is quite different from the Renaissance posture of "doubt based on pride." Rather it respects the mystery of human existence without trying to unravel or explain it away in some kind of all-encompassing world-view.

The other kind of secularization, and the one most often intended by the term, Gogarten calls "secularism." It arises when the questioning ignorance in regard to the idea of wholeness is not maintained and one gives up either his ignorance or his questioning.[23] Gogarten describes two types of secularism, corresponding to these two perversions of secularization. When the *ignorance* is denied and ultimate meaning is ascribed to man himself, he claims to provide his own wholeness in what Gogarten calls "modern subjectivism" or "ideology." He shows how both idealism and Marxism claim that man himself is the source of meaning for all existence.[24] When the *questioning* is considered fruitless and all questions of meaning are thought to be answered within the visible, a realism or positivism results which often leads to nihilism and the abandonment of any search for wholeness.[25]

Secularization degenerates into "secularism" when from either side this tension is relaxed. It occurs when improper claims are made for faith, either as a metaphysical world-view or ecclesiastical pattern for control of the state, sciences, education, or morals. It also results when an effort is made to eliminate the "religious" or to close off the secular from faith.

Although he speaks repeatedly of "two very different kinds of secularization," Gogarten's designation of the second kind which cuts itself off from faith as "*erroneous* secularization" or "secularism" indicates that there is, in his mind, only one *true* secularization. Perhaps this is but another way of underscoring the fact that secularization is always to be understood as a dynamic process. If and when it becomes an end or an established condition, a philosophy or a world-view, it surrenders the necessary tension which produced it and "degenerates" into secularism. The former remains a relative, dialectic tension, whereas the latter becomes an absolutized, static point of view.[26]

Yet if secularization so conceived is a necessary and legitimate consequence of Christian faith which is always in danger of degenerating into secularism, Gogarten feels constrained to make clear the relation between faith and secularization today. The failure of theology and the church to understand this relation is "the misfortune of the modern age," Gogarten feels, for they seek "to preserve in the Christian faith what reason has long since given over to the genuine direction of the human."[27]

> So long as faith and secularization remain what they are according to their nature, the relation between them cannot be one of contending with each other for the sphere belonging to them. If faith means keeping from secularization what is seized by it, faith ceases to be faith. If secularization begins to claim for itself that which belongs

to faith, secularization does not remain within secularity, but becomes secularism. The task faith has in regard to secularization, therefore, is to help it remain within secularity. But it can only fulfill this task when faith remains faith. It remains faith when it is distinguishing unceasingly between faith and works, between the divine reality of salvation and the earthly-worldly meaning of all human acts.[28]

This suggests that faith must expose itself continually to the secular world, not withdrawing from it, but remaining sympathetic to its historical problems and demands.

Gogarten believes that though there is no genuine faith which does not lead to such a secularization on the part of believers in relation to the world, there can be secularization without faith when it becomes cut off from faith in the freedom which was originally made available by faith. This happens, as noted above, when reason reaches out beyond questioning ignorance with its highest ideals, its limits, or when it no longer exposes itself to the uncertainty of the future. It also occurs whenever the attempt is made to give meaning to the whole on the basis of a part.

Faith must not only make the distinction which initiates secularization but also constantly safeguard it if secularization is not to deteriorate into secularism. It is secularism, not secularization, which threatens faith. This can take either a Christian form, such as "utopian secularism," which seeks to shape the world and reduces faith to answers; or "chronic secularism," which reduces the Christian faith to morals; or it can assume the pseudo-religious forms of ideology or nihilism. In either case, questioning ignorance which faith demands concerning ultimate meaning becomes subverted. This distinction between two forms of secularization, or more accurately, the *process of secularization,* which recognizes its source in faith and maintains a creative tension with it without seeking a premature resolution, and the *ideology of secularism,* which refuses to acknowledge its foundation and abandons its questioning ignorance by ascribing ultimate meaning to some partial or relative truth, is one of the most helpful contributions Gogarten has made to recent theological discussions of secularity. His distinction between "secularization" and "secularism" implies a common source and assumes that one may properly understand secularization and its consequences and guard against "erroneous secularization" only when aware of its Christian roots.

By designating the world "just world" and by making man free from it yet responsible for it, the Christian faith has shattered the meaning which was once self-evident to man in his enclosedness by the world. Now he can either accept the relationship to a received ultimate meaning revealed in faith or he can endeavor to create his own, becoming re-enslaved to "this world." The former involves living in a sense of mystery, searching in questioning ignorance for the meaning which has been revealed to man; the latter means ascribing ultimacy to some worldly meaning and resolving the tension in some comprehensive world-view.

H. Richard Niebuhr, following a cue from Stephen Pepper, developed the idea of "root-metaphors," or basic analogies which determine a person's concepts of explanation and description and eventually one's "world hypothesis."[29] Niebuhr suggests that in man's quest after knowledge of himself as agent he has pictured himself as man-the-maker and as man-the-citizen. He then argues that the emerging root-metaphor of modern man is responsibility, the image of man-the-answerer, including such elements as *response* to an *awareness* of action upon him, *interpretation* of what is being done to him, *accountability* for the consequences of his actions, and *involvement* with other persons with whom he is involved in continuing discourse and interaction.[30]

In any reading of Gogarten's later writings one is struck by his preoccupation with responsibility and the way it functions as the "root-metaphor" of his theology. Man is the being who cannot live except in responsibility; it is the law of his nature. This term has appeared in each of the areas we have examined, characterizing man's relation to the world as user, to God as son, and to history as participant. It functions, however, not as a moral or metaphysical term, but always as a historical category, loaded with the connotations of personal encounter, reciprocal relationship, answerability to God, and openness to the other.

Each of the conceptual models which Gogarten uses to provide epistemological vividness to this "root-metaphor" of responsibility shares this heuristic function, whether he is speaking of creaturehood (which entails a quite different relationship to the Creator than the relation of artwork to artist, machine to its designer, or the product to its manufacturer), sonship, or lordship. Each of these has a concrete, historical, and personal connotation, and each contains within it the correlative notion of freedom to be irresponsible by denying creatureliness, forfeiting sonship, neglecting the inheritance, or evading the obligations of lordship.

To depict the process of secularization as the increasing delegation and acceptance of responsibility of man for the ongoing life of the world is to see man's relationship to the world in the light of his relationship to God, to underscore the givenness of responsibility with humanness, and to view as perverted any effort to assert authority without recognizing its source or its relativity.

SECULARIZATION IN THE THOUGHT OF DIETRICH BONHOEFFER

The next step in this effort to understand how the concept of secularization functions in contemporary theology is to traverse the theological writings of Dietrich Bonhoeffer, seeking to discover how he considered ours a "world come of age" and to discover what part, if any, the Christian faith has had in this "movement toward the autonomy of man."

This is a stimulating step, suggesting, on the one hand, a world-affirming dimension of the Judeo-Christian tradition which sharply questions traditional distinctions between the sacred and the secular, temporal and eternal, religious and "irreligious" realms. At the same time, this movement into Bonhoeffer's thought is a frustrating one, for here one is confronted not only with a predilection against systematizing, but also a very incomplete, piecemeal, and impulsive theological enterprise. This fragmentariness should not be disparaged, however, but recognized as characteristic of this man who felt that the very fragmentariness of life "points towards a fulfillment beyond the limits of human achievement."[31]

Although there have been numerous efforts to extract from Bonhoeffer's writings only that which confirms previous notions about his view of Christ, the church, or the world, and thus to play the "earlier Bonhoeffer" against the "later Bonhoeffer," it is the intention of this study of his thought concerning secularization to examine those references in his writings which illumine the process which he described as "the world's coming of age." This will, quite obviously, mean focusing upon his *Ethics* and *Letters and Papers from Prison,* since in these his interest turned so explicitly to the world and man's relationship to it; but quotations from the earlier writings will be examined which prefigure and contribute to this final and unfinished movement in his theological symphony.

"The World Come of Age"

Although Bonhoeffer explicitly uses the term "secularization" on several occasions in his *Ethics*,[32] he more frequently refers to it as the process whereby the world and man have "come of age."[33]

His use of this phrase, by which Kant characterized the Enlightenment's effort to "release man from his self-incurred tutelage" and "lack of resolution and courage to use his reason without direction from another . . . external direction,"[34] has inevitably been misunderstood by some of his readers. Labeling this both presumptuous and naïve, they have thought such a term to include all of the liberal and optimistic assumptions which prevailed in the theology and philosophy of the Enlightenment. It is clear, however, that "mature" in no sense denotes "perfect" or "improved" in Bonhoeffer's usage, but rather "responsible," "accountable"; and the "world come of age" is one with its own integrity, a world in which human problems must be faced and dealt with on their own terms. In Bonhoeffer's thought, "the world come of age" functions as much more than a popular motto or pejorative label for a would-be self-sufficient historical period. Rather, it has the status of a theological formula, a suggestive symbol which gathers up and illumines several fundamental insights about our present situation, a symbol whose very ambiguity contributes to its power. To grasp the inferences symbolized by this phrase and thus his understanding of secularization, one must review Bonhoeffer's reading of the recent history of ideas in the West.

In his *Ethics* he describes the breaking up of the *corpus christianum* which led to the distinction between the *corpus Christi* and the world. This disintegration of the historical order of the West was expressed politically in the Peace of Westphalia at the end of the Thirty Years' War, the symbol of the "political disunity of the west which had resulted from the schism of faith."[35]

On the Protestant side the process thus instigated was rooted in Luther's doctrine of the two realms. This emancipation of the reason and sanctification of the natural led to the discovery of the "mysterious correspondence between the laws of thought and the laws of nature" which, combined with the desire for mastery over nature, led to the unparalleled rise of technology.

On the Roman Catholic side, the breakup of the *corpus christianum* took a more anti-clerical turn and expressed itself in the revolt against the church, emancipation of the masses, deification of nature, and absolutization of reason expressed philosophically in the French Encyclopedists and politically in the French Revolution.

In his letters from prison, Bonhoeffer seemed little concerned about the political implications of this movement, but saw it in larger terms as "one great development which leads to the idea of the autonomy of the world." In his view, the leading philosophers, theologians, and political theorists all recognized and gave expression to man's growing ability to get along by himself, apart from ecclesiastical control or metaphysical foundations. All contributed in one way or another to the process whereby the various disciplines now understand themselves on their own terms and have their own rules. The resulting world-view, in which the universe as a whole was removed from God's tutelage and science was removed from the supervision of theology, confined God first to the role of the creator (the

Deists' clockmaker) and then discovered that man no longer needed God even as a "working hypothesis." Religion remains, at the end of such a process, only a superfluous sphere on the edge of life, a supplement to reality for those who still desire it.

As a result of this process of displacing God and substituting human reasons for what were previously divine, revealed explanations, Bonhoeffer noted:

> There is no longer any need for God as a working hypothesis, whether in morals, politics or science. Nor is there any need for such a God in religion or philosophy (Feuerbach). In the name of intellectual honesty these working hypotheses should be dropped or dispensed with as far as possible. . . . the only way to be honest is to recognize that we have to live in the world *etsi deus non daretur*.[36]

This is the one side of the process of "coming of age" as Bonhoeffer understood it: the expansion of man's knowledge of the universe which renders unnecessary previous metaphysical explication and reduces the need for a God who serves as a "stop-gap" or escape mechanism, a deity whose existence is contingent upon man's incomplete knowledge or need for metaphysical explanations. Thus God is edged out of the world, banished to the boundaries of life, to a clearly defined "religious realm." There he meets the needs of those who are either intellectually dishonest and will not accept what has happened or not yet mature enough to live in the world without a God who serves as "the answer to life's problems, the solution to its distresses and conflicts." As a matter of fact, "knowledge and life are thought to be perfectly possible without him" now, for divine initiative, grace, has been replaced by human ability in the truly important areas of existence.

Yet the abandonment of the "god of explanation" and the emancipation of man from all religious authority are results of man's acceptance of responsibility for the world and the basis for hope, according to Bonhoeffer, since "the mature man cut off from God is addressable on the basis of his responsibility."

This suggests the other side of Bonhoeffer's interpretation of the "world come of age." He sees this not only as a process of "de-divinization" as man accepts responsibility for the autonomous orders of the world, but also as a process in which God "allows himself" to be edged out of the world in order to force us "to a true recognition of our situation in relation to God." Therefore, not only has man abandoned God, but the "world come of age" is also a world abandoned by God and left to its own devices.

> God is teaching us that we must live as men who can get along very well without him. The God who is with us is the God who forsakes us (Mark 15.34). The God who makes us live in this world without using him as a working hypothesis is the God before whom we are ever standing. Before God and with him we live without God. God allows himself to be edged out of the world and on to the cross. God is weak and powerless in the world, and that is exactly the way, the only way, in which he can be with us and help us. . . . The Bible . . . directs [us] to the powerlessness and suffering of God; only a suffering God can help. To this extent we may say that the process we have described by which the world came of age was an abandonment of a false conception of God, and a clearing of the decks for the God of the Bible, who conquers power and space in the world by his weakness.[37]

Precisely this sense of "God-forsakenness" and the apparent emptiness of the traditional ways of understanding or talking about God make it possible for man to relate to God as he truly is, Bonhoeffer contended. The decreasing need for God as a solution to our unsolved human problems is the result of God's intention to free man from the notion that he is at the disposal of man, a *deus ex machina* hovering about waiting to rescue him from the difficulties into which he has gotten himself.

Only when such a God dies or is rendered impotent (and in this sense "secularization" is a process of deicide) is man able to relate to God as he truly is, through the concrete revelation in Jesus Christ. Although "God is dead" in the sense of outdated metaphysical foundations, in the Christian community there is the confidence that Christ lives, that God has revealed himself in a completely relevant way within the life of the world.

However this process is viewed—as man's abandoning an unnecessary "divine hypothesis" or God's withdrawing from, or allowing himself to be abandoned by, a world increasingly responsible for itself—the result is the same, according to Bonhoeffer. Ours is a world which is "godless," forced to live as if there were no God. Here the process of secularization, or "becoming mature," is ascribed a divine origin and a divine purpose. It is regarded not as a threat to faith but an irreversible spiritual process which must be accepted and taken into account as the present context of faith.

Bonhoeffer's view of secularization as the process of increasing godlessness is further clarified by recognizing the twofold use he makes of the term "God." In one of his prison letters, Bonhoeffer described modern man learning "to cope with all questions of importance without recourse to God as a working hypothesis," and noted, "what we call 'God' is being more and more edged out of life."[38] The first use, without quotation marks, is a proper name, like Fred or John, one who is a presence, a meaning, who can be personally known. This is the God who acts in history and whose acts are recorded in the Scriptures, the one in Bonhoeffer's Christocentric theology who is present to us in Jesus Christ and in the concrete encounters "with the other nearest at hand" today. The second use, with quotation marks, is a descriptive title, an impersonal office or function designating a way of coping with certain needs or explaining certain occurrences.

Bonhoeffer had earlier made this same distinction in his commentary on the Second Commandment when he wrote,

> "God" for us is not a general concept with which we designate the highest, holiest, and mightiest that can be conceived. On the contrary, "God" is a name. When pagans say "God," they mean something completely different from what we mean when we, to whom God himself has spoken, say "God." For us, God is our God, the Lord, the Living One.[39]

Bonhoeffer is saying in effect that man's need for a "God" who can be used as an explanation is decreasing, opening up anew the possibility of knowing God as he truly is, the one revealed in Jesus Christ. Hence it is not threatening to faith that such godlessness abounds today, but evidence of a potential openness to the God of the Bible, who is not a general explanation or abstract hypothesis whose importance recedes in inverse proportion to man's maturity, but one who acts in a personal, concrete, and historical way in Jesus Christ. Dependence upon the former is illegitimate, a form of "intellectual dishonesty," the essence of "religion" as Bonhoeffer conceived it, whereas dependence upon and suffering in behalf of the latter is a legitimate dependence, the essence of faith.[40]

The new dimension in Bonhoeffer's appraisal of the "world come of age" and the response his writings have provoked among younger theologians stem from his claim that the church must accept the outcome of this process and recognize in it not an evil force to be overcome or a weakening of God's power, but a development willed by God and subject to human determination.

This "Religionless Age"

A second, closely related context in which Bonhoeffer's understanding of secularization emerges is his description of the decline of religion and the effort he made to disengage the Christian faith from a "religious interpretation," in his plea for a "worldly Christianity," and his hope to develop a "non-religious interpretation of biblical concepts."

Although the distinction between biblical faith and religion was already operative in some sense in the Old Testament tension between the prophetic and priestly traditions, in the New Testament tension between gospel and law, and in Luther's stress on *sola gratia, sola fide,* which set aside the "religious question" of self-justification, it was Karl Barth who sharpened this distinction in contemporary theology and it was from Barth that Bonhoeffer drew the impetus for his distinction.

The distinction which Barth makes between religion and Christian faith in his *Church Dogmatics* (Vol. I, Part 2) is primarily a distinction between self-justification and divinely initiated salvation, and it is possible to speak of Christianity as the "true religion," "preserved religion," only when it is recognized that it stands under the judgment of God and is formed and sustained by divine revelation. Faith must be expressed in religion, but any religion which seeks to provide explanations or to make man righteous apart from divine grace is just one religion among many and hence a form of idolatry and unbelief which is an offense to God.

It is here that Bonhoeffer departed from Barth, however, for he could not conceive of any religion which is *not* used by men to justify themselves in their immaturity. So, while Bonhoeffer acknowledged his indebtedness to Barth for his critique of religion, he deplored Barth's step back into what he called a "positivist doctrine of revelation" which sets up, in the final analysis, "a law of faith."[41] Making and maintaining a sharp distinction between religion and faith, Bonhoeffer pictured *religion* as any human activity to reach salvation or the postulation of a deity for help, protection, or explanation, in order to underscore the nature of *faith* as active participation in the suffering of the world which discerns God's presence in the "nearest Thou at hand."[42]

On the basis of this kind of distinction between faith and religion, Bonhoeffer could describe a "godlessness which is full of promise, which speaks against religion and against the church" in his *Ethics* and characterize the present as a "religionless age" in his letters from prison.

Although many subsequent works have explored or carried forward the sharp distinction between biblical faith and religion, it is important for this study to be quite clear how the term "religion" functions in Bonhoeffer's thought in order to understand the process of secularization as "de-religionization," or the disintegration of religion.

The first characteristic of religion as Bonhoeffer conceived it is its dichotomizing of reality into the sacred and the secular. Reacting against the misreading of Luther's doctrine of the two realms, he considered the concept of a "juxtaposition and conflict of two spheres, the one divine, holy, supernatural and Christian, and the other worldly, profane, natural and un-Christian" as foreign to the New Testament and "the colossal obstacle of a large part of traditional Christian ethical thought."[43]

He deplored this separation into two static and mutually exclusive spheres, for it forces man to abandon reality and to place himself in one or other of the two spheres, "seeking Christ without the world or the world without Christ." In this dichot-omized reality, religion becomes the antithesis of the secular, and as Nietzsche charged the Christians of his day, the resulting otherworldliness can be understood as nothing other than a hatred and contempt for the world, a desire to escape from it, and an irresponsibility toward life within it. J. A. T. Robinson describes the result as follows:

> The 'religious' . . . relates to that department of life which is contrasted with 'the world'; and in its popular non-technical sense it includes all those activities which go on within the circle of the sanctuary, whether literally or metaphorically. It is a particular area of experience or activity into which a man may turn aside or 'go apart', and which has its own psychology and sociology. A 're-ligious revival' means the burgeoning of this area of experience and activity, and the process of secularization its diminution or decline. And the Churches are universally assumed to have a vested interest in the former and to deplore the latter.
>
> It is this assumption against which Bonhoeffer is putting his question mark.[44]

Beginning with the Old Testament's world-affirming view and prophetic attack upon religiosity, biblical faith has pared away the dualistic categories, seeking to cut man off from the "re-ligious security of the mythological cosmos."

Religious otherworldliness, which depends upon the main-tenance of a rigid distinction between the sacred and the secu-lar, is disappearing, according to Bonhoeffer, in the light of the advance of the "genuine worldliness" made plain in the in-carnation of God in Jesus Christ and the "spurious worldliness" which "strives desperately and convulsively to achieve the deifi-cation of the worldly."[45]

Bonhoeffer also thought of religion as "metaphysics." "How do we speak of God without religion, i.e. without the tempo-rally-influenced presuppositions of metaphysics, inwardness, and so on?" he asked in his letter from prison of April 30, 1944. To speak religiously means to speak "metaphysically."[46] Since the term "metaphysics" has been variously understood and the meta-physical approach rejected for a variety of reasons in the recent history of philosophy, it is important to inquire just what Bonhoeffer intended with the term. Clearly he was not protesting against the confused linguistic assertions of religion, using "metaphysical" in the negative sense of the logical positivists. Nor did he reject metaphysics as a presumptuous misuse of reason, using the term in the negative sense of those theologians who pit faith against reason or reject all metaphysics as ontological and hence unhistorical and unbiblical. And although Bonhoeffer was conversant with Heidegger's early writings and discussed his interpretation of Being at length in *Act and Being*, there is no evidence that he ever used Heideggerian categories to characterize metaphysics as "an error into which thinking was misled by Being." Nevertheless, insofar as Bonhoeffer indicated that metaphysics is a postulation of God in subject-object terms as an explanation or working hypothesis which completes man's picture of the world and provides some sense of fixedness and security in it, it involves the same "philosophy of subjectivism" which Heidegger deplored.

Bonhoeffer was critical of any human mode of thought which sought to provide a religious escape from the world or a false security in the world on the basis of a fixed world-picture or circumscribed system of truth. His disdain was not on methodological grounds or in terms of the content of metaphysics as a threat to revelation or faith. Rather, he considered the attitude of religious "answer-seeking" or "system-building" to be contrary to faith, an effort, in Peter Berger's words, "to furnish a sacred cave, a religious meaning system within which one can hide from ambiguity."[47]

To the extent that man in a "world come of age" decreasingly tends to postulate an overarching scheme, a supernatural order above the natural, another world beyond this one, or a pretentious picture of the All, and has less and less need for a *deus ex machina*, religion as metaphysics is on the wane, according to Bonhoeffer.

A "time of religion" is also marked by its "inwardness and conscience." To speak religiously means to speak "individualistically."[48] Primarily, Bonhoeffer was describing the result of the "displacement of God" which narrows the "religious realm" where God is used as a "stop-gap" down to such personal problems as guilt, suffering, and death. This is the tendency of religion to make room for God "on the borders of human existence." Here he deplored the predilection of existential philosophy, psychotherapy, and pastoral counseling to exploit individual weakness and insecurity in order to prepare the way for the postulation of God as comfort in human failure, the answer to the problems of life.

Such attacks by Christian apologetics upon the self-assurance of men or the adulthood of their world Bonhoeffer considered a form of "religious coercion" which is

> in the first place pointless, in the second ignoble, and in the third un-Christian. Pointless, because it looks to me like an attempt to put a grown-up man back into adolescence, i.e. to make him dependent on things on which he is not in fact dependent any more . . . Ignoble, because this amounts to an effort to exploit the weakness of man for purposes alien to him and not freely subscribed to by him. Un-Christian, because for Christ himself is being substituted one particular stage in the religiousness of man, i.e. a human law.[49]

Besides, he had written a few days earlier, even when men's needs have been thus exposed,

> It just isn't true to say that Christianity alone has the answers. In fact the Christian answers are no more conclusive or compelling than any of the others. . . . Christ is the centre of life, and in no sense did he come to answer our unsolved problems.[50]

At the same time, Bonhoeffer was also referring to the individualistic concern for personal salvation in religion which often leads to the neglect of worldly responsibility. "It is not with the next world we are concerned, but with this world as created and preserved and set subject to laws and atoned for and made new."[51]

> . . . the Old Testament speaks of *historical* redemption, i.e. redemption on this side of death, whereas the myths of salvation are concerned to offer men deliverance from death. . . . The salvation myths deny history in the interests of an eternity after death. . . . The difference between the Christian hope of resurrection and a mythological hope is that the Christian hope sends a man back to his life on earth in a wholly new way which is even more sharply defined than it is in the Old Testament. . . . This world must not be prematurely written off. In this the Old and New Testaments are at one. Myths of salvation

arise from human experiences of the boundary situation. Christ takes hold of a man in the centre of his life.[52]

Such a religion, which addresses man "only in his weakness and meaninglessness" and feeds upon human desperation about individual inadequacies or anxiety about personal salvation after death, is becoming increasingly superfluous as death and sin seem no longer to be regarded as "genuine borderlines."

In all of these characterizations, Bonhoeffer made clear that religion represents a dispensable relationship of childlike dependence upon God, a failure to accept responsibility for the world he has turned over to man; thus his choice of the phrase "maturity" to describe man's present status in the world in contrast to "minority," a relationship in which God is viewed as guardian or anxious parent who is always on hand to answer human questions or right human wrongs, but remains, in effect, at man's disposal.

The "innate religious longing" is now seen by Bonhoeffer to be "an historical and temporary form of human self-expression," a status which is being outgrown as man learns to live in a "world come of age" without needing religion as a crutch.[53]

It is unfortunate that Bonhoeffer adopted so uncritically this Comte-like periodization of history, implying that the religious stage is automatically superseded by a rational or scientific one in which man no longer needs the "crutch of religion." This "nominal definition" of religion which he developed primarily as a way to provoke a new understanding of the Christian faith and his description of religion as a "passing stage" were not intended to be statements of fact as much as aids to recognition, evoking awareness of the understanding of God and the world which the Christian faith contains.

Nevertheless, if religion is defined as the human effort to "supplement reality by a god-hypothesis," then Bonhoeffer is not only provocative but accurate in observing that the period since the Enlightenment has seen a decreasing interest in religion and that man in the present age is distinguished by his self-confidence and distrust of traditional religious answers.

Just as the Apostle Paul made clear that circumcision was no longer a precondition for justification in the light of faith in his day, Bonhoeffer insisted that religion is no longer to be considered a precondition for salvation today.

On the basis of such a depreciation of religion—as false otherworldliness, outdated metaphysics, self-contained inwardness and hyperindividualism, and a passing stage in the world's "coming of age"—Bonhoeffer concerned himself with the question of how the Christian faith can be proclaimed in such a "religionless age." "How do we speak in a secular fashion of God?" He mentioned on several occasions the need for a "non-religious interpretation of biblical concepts" but provided only hints of what this might include, e.g.,

> . . . a new language, which will horrify men, and yet overwhelm them by its power. It will be the language of a new righteousness and truth, a language which proclaims the peace of God with men and the advent of his kingdom. . . . Until then the Christian cause will be a silent and hidden affair . . .[54]

Clearly more was intended here than Bultmann's program of demythologizing, for it is not just mythological forms but religious conceptions themselves which are problematic. Although there has been considerable effort to set down what was intended, perhaps his friend Eberhard Bethge has said all that can be said concerning Bonhoeffer's hope.

> Non-religious interpreting must do the opposite of what religious interpretation is doing: not making God the stop-gap of our insufficiencies, not relating the world in its misfits to a *deus ex machina*, but respecting its adulthood. The churches must not fight for the wrong causes, their religious and *weltanschauliche* dressing, for something which is not the cause of Jesus. . . . The church must not throw away its great terms 'creation', 'fall', 'atonement', 'repentance', 'last things', and so on. But if she cannot relate them to the secularized world in such a way that their essence in worldly life can immediately be seen, then the church had better keep silent.[55]

The substance of Bonhoeffer's provocative and fragmentary comments about religion is that this is an age in which religion as he characterized it is disappearing and apparently there is little or no need for a god of explanation. It would be easy indeed to take issue with Bonhoeffer's conclusion and, armed with religious surveys, statistics concerning church construction, publications, and membership, or functional definitions of religion, to prove him wrong. Surely there must always be some structure of meaning, some system of attitudes or ideology, some "common religion" which operates within a society to give it cohesion, whether based upon God, state, race, or a "way of life."[56] By defining religion as "ultimate concern," it can be shown that all men are ultimately concerned about something, even idolatrously ascribing ultimacy to that which is conditioned and relative.[57] Or again, one could acknowledge the possible validity of Bonhoeffer's claim as it applies to European religious life, but except the United States from his analysis, holding that the process he was describing has not yet reached fruition or become visible in this country.

But all of these would be to misunderstand the way the term "religion" functions in Bonhoeffer's thought. His was no statistical, analytical, or phenomenological investigation of religion; the figures on church membership or evidences of current religiosity neither prove nor disprove his point. Nor was he concerned about the operative or functional religion of his day. He was not seeking to define religion in any traditional way, according to content or belief, affect or feelings, practice or ethics. Rather, his was a provocative, "propagandistic"[58] definition which did not seek to do justice to all historical manifestations of the genre or to deny that when religion disintegrates, a variety of religious substitutes or ersatz religions emerge.

If one recalls the provocative way in which Bonhoeffer described religion, it becomes clear that he was using the faith-religion distinction which he had found in Karl Barth's theology to describe the radically new historical situation in which he saw European spiritual life. Instead of using this distinction as Barth does, however, and maintaining a dialectical tension between revelation and religion, between what God makes available to man and his institutionalized response, Bonhoeffer pushed it further into a "religionless" form in order to emphasize not simply the theological insight here but the change from the previous period when such a dialectic could be maintained. As he borrowed Kant's pseudo-philosophical characterization of the Enlightenment era and poured theological content into it, he borrowed Barth's theological critique of religion and poured historical and philosophical content into it, making it a symbol of the same process of secularization.

In this case, the designation of this as a "religionless age" is synonymous with the former label, "a world come of age," with as little precision used in describing the forces initiating the process as before. In short, this is Bonhoeffer's way of denoting that something radically different has happened within the past two centuries in man's understanding of his relation to the world and to God, leaving this not a pagan or un-Christian age, but an age which no longer seems to need religion for self-justification.

This is also his way of saying that the language, forms, and cultic acts in which the Christian faith has become enmeshed, with the concomitant defensiveness which religious institutions develop, make necessary a sharp distinction between the Christian faith as participation in the world and the religious forms of otherworldliness and piety which until recently provided an escape from the world. This is a distinction not unlike that between Christianity and Christendom in Søren Kierkegaard's *Attack on Christendom,* and made for precisely the same reasons.

And thirdly, the term "religionless age" functions as a symbol for the scientifically permeated, technologically advanced world which renders previous religious world-views irrelevant and requires the reiteration that the Christian faith is not a competitive world-view, either mythical, scholastic, or existentialist, but something radically different. Bonhoeffer seemed to feel that the desuetude of religion was not a thing to be decried, but in fact a promising opportunity to make clear the true nature of faith and the authentic relation to God. Since he viewed religion as seeking to impose illegitimate limits on human freedom to face the world, his talk of a religionless age was more normative than descriptive, more the result of theological commitment than empirical observation.

The first two descriptions of secularization as "coming of

age" and "de-religionization" have been symbols of "deck-clearing," the destruction of prevailing mythical and religious views. The other context in which the notion functions for Bonhoeffer is the constructive process in which the Christian faith is seen as making possible the recognition of the "relative autonomy of the world," that is, secularization as acceptance of genuine worldliness based upon the concrete historical revelation of God in Jesus Christ.

Genuine Worldliness

Reacting against those theological movements which were emphasizing the "wholly otherness" and uncompromising transcendence of God, and the passive attitude of certain German church leaders who ignored their secular responsibilities because of a static "two realm" doctrine, Bonhoeffer's whole theological enterprise was an effort to repudiate a false "spirituality" and to explore the concreteness of revelation in its tangible, particular, and historical sense. In an address delivered in 1932, he had described the coming of Christ as "an affirmation of the earth, and entrance into its orders, its communities, its history."[59]

> Ever since we worked out the evil device of being religious—yes, even Christian—at the expense of the world, we have been otherworldly. Otherworldliness is a very pleasant state to live in. Whenever life begins to become painful and importunate, you can leap into the air and ascend unburdened and unconcerned to the so-called eternal fields. You ignore the present; you despise the world because you are superior to it . . .[60]

In contrast to most of the other dialectic theologians of this period, who insisted that the finite cannot contain the infinite, Bonhoeffer assumed that the distinctive Lutheran understanding of the incarnation could be interpreted in such a way as to safeguard God's transcendence while emphasizing that it is *this* world which God created, pronounced good, and redeemed in Jesus Christ.

This he sought to do in his stress upon the concreteness of revelation, ethics as the "setting free of life for genuine worldliness," and God's "this-worldly transcendence." Always the "better secularity" which the Christian faith makes possible is rooted in concrete involvement in the world expressed by God in Jesus Christ.

> Just as in Christ the reality of God entered into the reality of the world, so, too, is that which is Christian to be found only in that which is of the world, the 'supernatural' only in the natural, the holy only in the profane, and the revelational only in the rational. . . . And yet what is Christian is not identical with what is of the world. The natural is not identical with the supernatural or the revelational with the rational. But between the two there is in each case a unity which derives solely from the reality of Christ, that is to say solely from faith in this ultimate reality.[61]

What is revealed in these penultimate forms, however, is not God's omnipotence or power but his concrete concern. Talk of God's majesty is too general and abstract, just a partial extension of the world.

> Our relation to God [is] not a religious relationship to a supreme Being, absolute in power and goodness, which is a spurious conception of transcendence, but a new life for others, through participation in the Being of God. The transcendence consists not in tasks beyond our scope and power, but in the nearest Thou at hand. God in human form, not . . . in abstract form—the absolute, metaphysical, infinite, etc.—nor yet in the Greek divine-human of autonomous man, but man existing for others, and hence the Crucified.[62]

The implications of this emphasis upon the concreteness of revelation in Jesus Christ and "this-worldly transcendence" in which man perceives God's presence in the midst of historical human existence are several. In regard to the world, it means the rejection of any concept of two autonomous orders or any attempt to restrict faith to the realm of individual response, by asserting that Christ's sovereignty embraces the whole world.

In regard to the self, the incarnation of God as man means that now man knows what true manhood is like and is able to become man. We are constituted as persons and become authentic selves only as we are confronted by and become involved with the other. ". . . in view of the incarnation of God, to live as man before God can mean only to exist not for oneself but for God and for other men."[63]

> While we are trying to grow out beyond our manhood, to leave the man behind us, God becomes man and we have to recognize that God wishes us men, too, to be real men. . . . He leads us *ad absurdum*

> by Himself becoming a real man and a companion of sinners and
> thereby compelling us to become the judges of God. God sides with
> the real man and with the real world against all their accusers. . . .
> Man becomes man because God became man.[64]

Bonhoeffer contended that because Jesus was not primarily a
teacher or legislator, but first of all a man, he illustrated no particular doctrine or set of propositions, he championed no special religious practices, but rather called men to be men. And to
be a man requires for Bonhoeffer "participation in the suffering
of God in the life of the world."[65] It also means accepting responsibility for the world in its natural, penultimate form, for it
views all of life as *negotium cum deo*.

Thus in regard to human responsibility, the concrete revelation of God in Jesus Christ means acceptance of the "orders of
preservation" or "mandates" of natural life which God created
and by which he seeks to preserve life. It requires using the
reason, the organ of knowledge of the natural and itself part of
this preserved form of life, to perceive whatever presents itself.

It means relating to the world "as one who receives the com-
mission and power of his dominion from God." But responsibility involves freedom as well as obedience, and the only true
proof of a man's freedom is the fact that "nothing can answer
for him, nothing can exonerate him, except his own deed and
his own self. It is he himself who must observe, judge, weigh
up, decide and act."[66] Where this necessary tension between
obedience and freedom is resolved and we become disobedient
or, sacrificing our freedom to technology, become a slave of the
world, then "the earth is no longer *our* earth, and then we become strangers on earth."[67]

In his *Ethics* Bonhoeffer described responsibility in the world
as "deputyship," in which "man is directly obliged to act in the
place of other men," and as action "in accordance with reality,"
in which man does not impose an alien law upon reality but sets
it free for genuine worldly service. "Action which is in accordance with Christ is in accordance with reality because it allows
the world to be the world; it reckons with the world as the
world; and yet it never forgets that in Jesus Christ the world is

loved, condemned and reconciled by God."[68] Responsibility also includes what Bonhoeffer called "pertinence," a relationship toward the domain of things in which one presses to find "their original, essential and purposive relation to God and to man" and to discover the particular inherent law of being by which a thing exists.

Since the aim of the dominion of Christ is not to subject the worldly order to the church or to any unnatural law but "to set it free for true worldliness," the Christian has no desire to deprive secular institutions of their responsible decisions, but rather seeks to help them act responsibly in their "relative autonomy," i.e., autonomy in relation to all earthly heteronomies. They are not autonomous in relation to the law of Christ, for all reality is founded upon him.

> The dominion of Christ and the decalogue do not mean that the secular institutions are made subservient to a human ideal or 'natural law', nor yet to the Church . . . but they mean their emancipation for true worldliness, for the state to *be* a state, etc. The primary implication for secular institutions of the dominion of Christ and of the decalogue is not, therefore, the conversion of the statesman or the economist, nor yet the elimination of the harshness and unmercifulness of the state for the sake of a falsely interpreted christianization of the state and its transformation into a part of the Church. It is precisely in the dispensation of strict justice and in the administration of the office of the sword, in maintaining the unmerciful character of the institutions of the state, that is to say, their genuine worldliness, that the dominion of Christ, *i.e.* the rule of mercy, is given its due.[69]

The "genuine worldliness" which results from recognition that participation in the reality of Christ requires active participation in the life of the world is defined, therefore, as "taking life in one's stride, with all its duties and problems, its successes and failures, its experiences and helplessness."[70] It involves liberation for life in the world because it frees one from any need to deify the world or man, or to be bound to the world. Left to its own devices, the worldly element always seeks to deify itself, falling victim to a "spurious and incomplete worldliness." "Genuine" or "complete worldliness" is possible only in the recognition that God has overcome the division, tension, and conflicts between the "Christian" and "secular" elements. Only in faith is the freedom and courage available to allow "the world to be what it really is before God, namely, a world which in its godlessness is reconciled with God."[71]

Faith recognizes that the work of Christ frees the orders of creation for the fulfillment of their allotted functions and effects the reconciliation of what was previously disunited. Bonhoeffer was depicting an interpretation of reality in the light of the incarnation, not a pantheistic view of the identity of God and world in which God is somehow dissolved in the world. He was just as opposed to intraworldly as to extraworldly concepts of God.

By distinguishing between genuine and spurious worldliness, he recognized the constant temptation of the secular orders to absolutize themselves, to claim an autonomy from the basic reality of God as well as from other worldly structures, to close themselves to experiences of reality or recognition of truth in other areas.

To insure a genuine worldliness and to keep it from turning into spurious worldliness requires the maintenance of a dialectic between negation and affirmation, between "the 'yes' of creation, atonement and redemption, and the 'no' of the condemnation and death of the life which has fallen away from its origin, its essence and its goal."[72] For the Christian there is also a dialectic tension between the ultimate and the penultimate, one of the most important contributions of Bonhoeffer's "ethic of formation."

Rejecting any relationship of mutual exclusiveness between what is ultimate and what is penultimate—any sectarianism in which the penultimate is destroyed by the ultimate or any compromise (culture religion) in which the ultimate is excluded from the domain of the penultimate—he insisted that the "ultimate has become real in the cross, as the judgement upon all that is penultimate, yet also as mercy towards that penultimate which bows before the judgement of the ultimate."[73] The penultimate he defined as "everything that precedes the ultimate, everything that precedes the justification of the sinner by grace alone, everything which is to be regarded as leading up to the last thing *when the last thing has been found*."[74]

He described the process within the past two hundred years

in which "last things" have been increasingly called into question, pointing out that this has imperiled the stability of the penultimate. "What must be done, therefore, is to fortify the penultimate with a more emphatic proclamation of the ultimate, and also to protect the ultimate by taking due care for the penultimate."[75] Whereas "genuine worldliness" maintains this dialectic tension, always taking seriously the penultimate but seeing it in relationship to the ultimate, spurious forms of worldliness or secularism ignore this distinction and ascribe ultimacy to what is, in fact, penultimate because they have sacrificed the perspective which makes this dialectic possible and necessary.

In Bonhoeffer's scattered references to a "genuine worldliness" which affirms and protects the secularity of the world and the relative autonomies of its various orders, the concept of secularization assumes specific theological and Christological connotations. Here the term functions as a designation for increasing openness to and acceptance of the worldliness of the world based upon the correspondence of its reality with the reality revealed by God in Jesus Christ. This includes not simply an attitude toward the world and its various orders, but a program for relating to the world, becoming involved in it, helping to fulfill its inherent possibilities, and guarding it against the kind of absolutization and resulting disunity which ignores the reconciling work of God in Jesus Christ.

In this setting, the process of secularization was described as it was in order to get those who claim to know the meaning of the incarnation to recognize its secular implications and also to remind them of the limitations which such a position sets upon the externally imposed authority of the church, the imperialism of theology, or the presumed omniscience of individual Christians who would impose their "Christian answers" upon the various orders of the world. Thus Bonhoeffer's is a philosophical assertion about the nature of the world corresponding to the reality of God revealed in Christ; it is also an ethical assertion about participation in the being of Christ demanding servanthood in relation to other persons and involvement in their sufferings; and it is a theological assertion about the nature of divinity, understood here not in terms of God's exaltation and power, but in terms of Christ's humiliation, lowliness, and suffering with and for others.

Bonhoeffer's practice of juxtaposing traditionally contradictory terms like "religionless Christianity," "hopeful godlessness," "genuine worldliness," "this-worldly transcendence," and "better secularity" is illustrative not only of his provocative style but of the changed understanding of religion, God, world, transcendence, and the secular which he wished to emphasize. Although such phrases are susceptible both to initial misunderstanding and subsequent superficial sloganizing, they are consistent with his concern to provoke a radical reassessment of the relation of the church to the world and to evoke a new understanding of the Christian faith's responsibility to help persons become truly human in the "world come of age."

Whereas secularization seen as "coming of age" and "de-religionization" can be readily understood and does not require any faith commitment, this third description of the process whereby man accepts his worldliness presupposes a particular interpretation of the Christian faith, even a particular Christology. In the first two instances, the process of secularization involved the taking over of certain Christian insights by the world. This third characterization is the unique possession of those who hold this understanding of faith and remains basically enigmatic to an outsider.

Yet in all three contexts, secularization is seen neither as the result of man's guilty alienation from God nor as a consequence of some inevitable historical development, but as a religious-historical process in which the spiritual destiny of modern man is being fulfilled. Bonhoeffer's unique contribution was his analysis of secularization against a Christological background. His is a positive assessment of secularization, for he conceived of it as an abandonment of a false conception of God and hence as "a clearing of the decks for the God of the Bible," the end of a period of religious tutelage and guardianship, and a new openness to the world viewed in the light of the reality of God in Jesus Christ.

Although secularization may continue to threaten and invoke the ire of those churchmen who see it as a demonic movement, Bonhoeffer portrayed it as a "necessary and positive counterpoint in God's symphony." The positive evaluation of reason and science as means by which man assumes responsibility for the world which is turned over to him, and the negative assessment of self-justifying religion as that which obstructs responsible selfhood and authentic faith—all give to the reinterpretation of secularization a relevance beyond the community of believers and suggest new ways for relating the Christian faith to higher education.

CHAPTER 3

Secularization
Defined and Refined

To explore the meaning of a concept and assess its usefulness in providing new understanding requires more than exposition of how it functions in certain contemporary theological contexts. Therefore, the contention that the theological reinterpretation of secularization provides a suggestive way of reassessing certain developments in higher education and relating religion to secular universities in the future requires further refinement of this concept and exploration of the changes it denotes in Western thought. Only then will it be possible to use the concept as the basis for reviewing the development of higher education in America and for inquiring into the responsibility of Christians in relation to this process in the future.

In the preceding chapter, it became clear that the theological discussion of secularization does not use the kind of putative description which can be tested as to truth or falsity. Rather, its contexts indicated that this term is being used as a theological symbol for the radical transformation which has occurred in Western man's understanding of the world, God, and himself. In this sense, the term can be evaluated only as to adequacy and inclusiveness, that is, its ability to provoke a deeper awareness of the change in our relationship to the world and religious tradition and a new understanding of the process in which the world can be known as "just world" (Gogarten) and God can be known as "truly God" and not a concept or explanation in the service of man (Bonhoeffer).

Secularization
as the Alteration in Man's Attitude Toward the World

The effort to unpack the meaning of the concept of secularization in recent theological discussions disclosed that it contains a number of constituent notions, foremost of which is the transformation in man's understanding of the world and his relationship to it. In Gogarten's thought, this is described as the radical shift from the mythical world of the Greeks to the historical world of modern man; from the world viewed as *ordered cosmos*, whose self-evident harmony required that man adapt himself as a part to that whole, to the world viewed as *contingent structure*, in which man is now responsible for maintaining its form and order. The animism of earlier Greek thought, which failed to distinguish between God and nature and tended to think of nature as "ensouled" and hence deserving of man's awe and contemplation, was modified somewhat by the rationalism of later Greek thought with its effort to participate through reason in the perfect world of forms and ideas, its interest in changeless and eternal Being and disdain for the contingent and material. In contrast to this, the present attitude considers the world as problematic, not mysterious, as an objectified reality to be examined, questioned, understood, and then utilized by man.

Bonhoeffer contrasted not the Greek and modern views of the world, but rather the religious and nonreligious views. He described the religious man as one who regards the world as evil or incomplete and seeks to supplement reality with otherworldly hopes or a religious realm separate from the worldly. In contrast is the man who sees the world as the concrete, historical context of human existence where what is transcendent and ultimate can be experienced only in the midst of the worldly and penultimate.[1]

In both cases, the secularized view of the world is one which takes the world seriously, on the one hand, yet not as divine or sacred, on the other. It is the result of a process in which the cosmos has been de-divinized, stripped of its occult powers, and made available to man in a way previously inconceivable.

Although it is easy enough to find agreement that something quite radical has occurred in man's understanding of the world—reflected, for example, in our ambiguous use of words like "cosmos," "nature," and "universe"—and few would take exception to the before and after pictures used above to denote this process, it is described in quite different ways by most historians. Alexandre Koyré characterizes this transformation as

> the substitution for the conception of the world as a finite and well-ordered whole . . . that of an indefinite or even infinite universe no longer united by natural subordination, but unified only by the identity of its ultimate and basic components and laws; and the replacement of the Aristotelian conception of space—a differentiated set of inner-worldly places—by that of Euclidean geometry—an essentially infinite and homogeneous extension—from now on considered as identical with the real space of the world.[2]

Ernst Cassirer described it as the setting aside of the question of transcendence, in which nature ceases to be "mysterious and unknowable" and becomes "an organic whole, self-supporting and self-explanatory."[3] Or again, it has been depicted as a shift from interest in *why,* in final causes, to preoccupation with the question of *how,* the manner of causation, marked by a "general transference of interest from metaphysics to physics, from the contemplation of Being to the observation of becoming, from concern for final causes and Form to efficient causes and Matter."[4]

However this movement is described, it is clear that man's understanding of the world has undergone a radical change, from an enclosing sacred nature or a cosmos permeated by mind and drawn toward its fulfillment by final causes to a historical world of human relationships, no longer explicable in substantialistic categories. Whereas before, man was always seen in relation to the world which in some sense defined him, now the world is seen in relation to man, deriving its meaning from him.

To what can we attribute this radical change in man's attitude toward the world? Although some ascribe it to a "bold stride toward a freer and fuller rationality, unrestrained by arbitrary barriers,"[5] or to a growing impatience with inadequate theological explanations which simply did not do justice to the observable facts about the world (a view similar to Bonhoeffer's description of the "displacement" of the god-hypothesis), or to a "recoil from the inflexible rationality of medieval thought,"[6] Gogarten insists that the changed view of the world which underlies the rise of modern science and the shift from the

Ptolemaic-Aristotelian cosmology to the Newtonian and eventually the Einsteinian world-views arose in large part from the biblical doctrine of creation. As we have seen, it is belief in God as creator which de-divinizes the world and makes it "just world," an object worthy of man's investigation.

Although others have shared this conviction that the doctrine of creation is a basic assumption of modern science, few have made this case with more rigor than the late Michael Foster of Oxford. In three separate articles, Foster traced the factors which differentiate modern science from Greek natural science back to the biblical view of creation.[7] Insisting that "every doctrine of God contains or implies a doctrine of the world," he argued that only by the assertion that the world is created could the Greek deification of natural powers and natural objects be overcome. Only the extirpation of the concept of God as the parent of nature under the impact of the Christian doctrine of God as creator (Artificer) could overcome the notion that nature possesses within itself the same power by which it was produced. And only the ascription to God of freedom, an arbitrary faculty of will creating a contingent world, could overcome the two Greek assumptions of the "unreality of matter" and the "intelligibility of form" and rescue science from purely a priori contemplation. Creative activity in God, material substance in nature, empirical methods in modern science—these are the basic presuppositions of science for which the biblical understanding of creation is largely responsible, according to Foster.

Within the doctrine of creation is the view of the world as depopulated of spirits and occult powers, hence no longer mysterious, threatening, and enclosing; as containing regularity and order, hence worthy of study and capable of description and generalization; and as contingent, hence requiring investigation.

The Christian faith also contributes to the process of secularization as revision in man's attitude toward the world by its doctrine of incarnation. In Jesus Christ, who gives meaning to the models of sonship and lordship, man is able to see himself in a new relation to the world.

Bonhoeffer contended that the incarnation not only demonstrated *that* God intends for man to participate fully in the world, but also *how* he is to be truly human within it, in obedience, sharing in the sufferings of others. God's concrete, historical presence in the world in Jesus Christ thus changes the way man views the world and his authentic existence within it.

The emphasis upon responsibility to God in and for the world is another theological insight which contributes to a different attitude toward the world. Such responsibility includes not simply the demand to examine and understand the world and its laws in "questioning ignorance" but also the obligation to participate in its social structures, to seek for meaning in its penultimate forms.

In his description of the Puritans' "systematic, rational, and empirical study of nature for the glorification of God and his works," sociologist Robert K. Merton illustrates this. He describes the combination of rationalism and empiricism which was so pronounced in the Puritan ethic, and the process by which these soon came to be considered "independent means of ascertaining even religious truths." As evidence that the "Protestant ethic involved an attitudinal set favourable to science and technology," he cites the predominently Puritan membership of the Royal Society, the science courses available in the English Dissenting Academies and at Harvard as a result of Puritan influences, and the openness of the Pietist universities in Germany (Halle, Königsberg, and Göttingen) to the "new science." Concludes Merton:

> The positive estimation by Protestants of a hardly disguised utilitarianism, of intra-mundane interests, of a thorough-going empiricism, of the right and even duty of *libra examen*, and of the explicit individual questioning of authority was congenial to the very same values found in modern science . . . plus an active ascetic drive which necessitated the study of nature that it might be controlled.[8]

Needless to say, other intellectual historians have found no such incentive for research or worldly responsibility in traditional Christian thought, insisting that it was in spite of rather than because of the Christian faith that man was able to overcome the primitive view of the world as divine or the medieval view of the world as material and therefore evil. Nevertheless, within the biblical understanding of creation and incarnation are insights which contributed to this change in attitude toward the world. One historian of science summarizes these insights as follows:

> . . . modern science began as, in a sense, a Christian protest against Greek notions about the external world, and there is much in modern science which is in essential harmony with Christian faith: delight in the natural world because God made it; conviction that there is no ultimate dualism of good and evil, rationality and irrationality, in nature, because God is One and His creation is good; humility before the facts of nature because God meets us in the facts of every experience of life; a certain valid detachment from nature, because we do not fear nature or worship her, we fear and worship her God . . . confidence in men's ability to use nature for the service of man, because we have been given dominion over the creatures and over the earth; these are the values which some Christians have always found in science, and they are the values scientists will recognize as the contribution of their craft to the achievements of mankind.[9]

Although in the incarnation of Jesus Christ the world became a different world than it was before and man was made responsible for it by his restored "sonship," this worldlilization remained virtually submerged beneath the otherworldliness of Gnostic thought. According to Gogarten, the papal claims to spiritual-political worldly power during the Constantinian era, the medieval transformation of faith from encounter with the Word of God into acceptance of eternal verities, and from adherence to Jesus Christ into assent to propositions, and the efforts of Protestant scholasticism to turn the Christian faith into a rational world-view based upon an inerrant view of Scripture—all contributed to the blurring of the Pauline teachings about sonship, the world, and faith, and Luther's restatement of the same themes.

In Bonhoeffer's view, man's appropriation of this radically different view of the world was hindered by the various religious ideas which infected Christian thought, for example, the use of God as a "working hypothesis" or causal explanation in medieval thought, and the use of the religious or otherworldly realm as an escape from this world in "pietistic" thought. The movement in the late Renaissance and Enlightenment which began to free men from using God as First Cause or final explanation furthered this process of secularization. Every effort to keep man dependent upon an overarching scheme or metaphysical world-view prevented him from seeing the world as it really is before God. "Holy worldliness" became a viable alternative only after religious "holy otherworldliness" was brought into question by a growing impatience with efforts to view the world as different from what it is.

Various human attempts to achieve satisfying total explanations further retarded this development or led to its perversion, Gogarten insists. In order to be "just world," the world must have unity and wholeness. Yet the biblical understanding of creation recognizes that this wholeness comes not out of the world itself but from God in faith. In receiving from God its wholeness, the world is seen to be what it always was, God's creation, as well as a historical reality which is in the process of becoming. If either of these insights is lost—either the world's derivedness and ultimate wholeness, or its historical openness and relativity—then the dynamic tension within secularization is sacrificed. Man then denies the mystery of the world's wholeness, grounding its form and order in himself (as did speculative idealism), or seeks to ground it in the factual necessities of the world (as did Marxism).[10]

Thus conceived, the process of secularization was furthered by the breakdown of the total world-view of the Middle Ages and the shift from speculative teleological explanations to demonstrable efficient explanations. It becomes synonymous with the development of modern science. As long as science keeps as its object an experienceable part and makes no claim to provide ultimate wholeness and meaning, it preserves its "faithlessness," its secularity, and thus honors God. Only when it ceases searching for meaning in its particular area and succumbs to the demand for unity by claiming ultimate wholeness or meaning on the basis of its partial truths does science advocate a worldview. What was a valid secular method for investigating particular truths is then turned into an ideology, scientism. Only when science is reminded of its limits is its secularity preserved and it is kept from perversion into scientism, an ideology claiming to provide ultimate meaning.

Other examples of the perversion of the process of secularization as alteration in man's view of the world come readily to mind. In this context, romanticism can be understood as a re-divinization of nature, scientistic naturalism as the substitution of nature for God,[11] utilitarianism as exploitation of the world without any awareness of its source or sense of responsibility to its Creator, and empiricism as an attempt to absolutize a method and "convert the world of empirical actuality into a self-subsistent ultimate."[12]

Characteristic of the secularized view of the world is the absence of any sense of mystery or wonder. Beginning with Newton's contention that the world is rational throughout, and furthered by Descartes's obsession with clarity and distinctness, the notion that what is mysterious is "weird, occult, magic, or superstitious" has displaced the Greek and biblical views of mystery as something whose meaning must be revealed.[13] Hence the scientific method is often regarded as "problem-solving" and secular education seems dedicated to diminishing or obliterating mystery.

Secularization is here viewed as the removal of mystery, the tendency of the secularized mind to consider that which is not easily understood as merely unsolved but solvable problems. Gogarten's concern for preserving the mystery of the world, his insistence that human reason is never able to provide ultimate answers or to reach beyond a questioning ignorance, and the open-endedness of his understanding of history—all represent his desire to protest the banishment of wonder in a secularized world.

In contrast to those who contend that the technological spirit inevitably exploits rather than continues the quest for knowledge about the world, or bemoan the development of technical society and urge withdrawal and nonparticipation in its objectivizing structures, this insistence that the world has actually been placed in man's hands makes impossible any such depreciation of technology per se, while recognizing the possibility of the perversion of man's sovereignty vis-à-vis nature. As one student of modern technology has observed:

> . . . the fact is that grinding poverty, incessant work, widespread debilitating disease, lifelong hunger, and early death pinch man's spirit

and rob him of real freedom by limiting his possible choices to the single issue of survival. By lessening these common evils technology has opened to the mass of Western men the possibility of freedom, of a larger life in which justice, friendship, political freedom, and esthetic enjoyment are real options. . . . It may be that the freedom which a technological social order gives to man is hard to bear—as Dostoevski's Grand Inquisitor was at pains to point out. Yet man's new burden of loneliness and compartmentalization may be the birth pangs of his emergence as a new free man. . . . By freeing man from a constant, fearful attention to daily survival, from the institution of slavery, and from conformity to an ancestral identity, technology made possible for man some measure of that freedom which we discovered in Jesus of Nazareth.[14]

Elsewhere, the same writer has described the technological spirit as not only bringing modern man a larger measure of freedom than he has ever known, but also evidencing a tough humility, expectant openness and radical submission to facts, buoyant affirmation of the world, and playful delight in life.[15] Yet he warns,

This is not to deny the dark side of its power when distorted. The freedom it offers becomes slavery when its intense purposefulness inhibits man's ability to hold functionally ambiguous ends. Humility can become arrogance when technology is linked with that bright, doctrinaire, dogmatic rationalism that refuses to accept the pragmatic weight of, say, poetry or love. And its affirmation of life, when confined by that same limiting rationalism, can destroy the richness of human life.[16]

In summary, it appears that secularization theologically understood denotes that process whereby men have moved from a view of the world as mysterious and demon-filled nature or substantial and self-explanatory cosmos to a view of the world as the realm of historical existence, to be studied, explored, and experienced. Although this is a process traceable to the biblical understanding of creation and incarnation and the notion of worldly responsibility which is derived from the Christian faith, it has prompted scientific research, technological development, and political and economic reforms which do not necessarily acknowledge their debt to these insights.

Wherever men no longer worship the world, neither living in fear of it nor ascribing a mysterious divine power to it, and wherever men accept responsibility for studying, understanding, and preserving the order of the world—there secularization, thus conceived, has taken place. Wherever men have assumed that the world is their natural possession and depend upon human effort for ultimate wholeness and purpose, or have opposed the development of experimental science, belittled the "penultimate" in behalf of the "ultimate," and felt their faith threatened by the discovery of new truth—there the process of secularization has been short-circuited by the absolutizing of the relative on the one hand, or by the perversion of faith into ideology on the other. The risk in creation, therefore, is that man will seek to live unto himself, attempting to be god, instead of accepting his mature sonship and viewing his life in the world as responsibility to God.

Secularization
as the Transformation of Man's Attitude Toward Truth

The second major alteration symbolized by the term "secularization" is in man's understanding of reality and his relationship to it. Cornelis van Peursen, one of the more able spokesmen for the recent Dutch discussion of secularization, has traced this radical reorientation in human thought through three stages, closely paralleling the changing view of the world just described.[17] In the "stage of myth" nature itself is supernatural, for numinous forces are everywhere. Mythical thinking is largely fascination *that* something is. In the "stage of ontology," man becomes a subject searching for being as being. The danger of this ontological stage is "substantialistic thought," or the isolation of substances, thinking of things in themselves.

The third stage van Peursen describes as the secular age, the "period of functional thought," in which reflection is not upon isolated substances, but becomes rather a tool of concrete human lives. Whereas in the period of myth, the primary concern was *that* something is, and in the stage of ontology, *what* something is, in this present period, it is *how* something is, *how* it functions for man, posing the danger in the secular age of "operational thinking" in which "the subject again becomes autonomous. . . . the object is merely the operation of the subject."

Although such a description of the changes in human thought is too facile and recalls a Comtean fondness for neat periodizations (noted earlier in Bonhoeffer's talk of our "religionless age") which overlook the continued existence of mythical and ontological thought in a "functional age," van Peursen is depicting the same dismantling of classical ontology and substantialistic metaphysics which Gogarten and Bonhoeffer saw as part of the process of secularization, and the correlative change in the status of theology and the role of reason this entailed.

Although some have defined secularization as "de-metaphysicalization," such a simplistic designation scarcely does justice to the ambiguity surrounding the current use of the term "metaphysics."[18] If metaphysics is used in the least technical sense as "talk about transcendent and unobservable entities,"[19] then the issue is not simply whether a man thinks metaphysically, but the nature of the model he uses. Is it the naturalistic one of classical metaphysics with its analysis of being as substance and accident, or the rationalistic model of "logical metaphysics" with its deductions from a priori principles, or the dramatic model of "existential metaphysics" with its historical understanding of being? Equally important is the status ascribed to metaphysical formulations, whether they are considered absolute and universally self-evident or relative and open to criticism as to their consistency and applicability to experience.[20] The process of secularization seems to involve the decline of the first of these, classical metaphysics, and the loss of power of that rigid and static view of things which was considered self-evident down to the late eighteenth century.

Other writers have depicted this alteration as the eventual triumph of a "metaphysic of self-consciousness" over a "metaphysic of nature,"[21] as a shift in thought "from definition to description, from the species to the individual,"[22] from a conception of nature which seeks to derive and explain becoming from being to the derivation of being from becoming, and as "the transition from the notion that truth has been delivered in the past and is to be uncovered and recovered in every age to the view that truth is fundamentally to be discovered or that it lies in the future."[23] The same movement is reflected in the change from the fixed curriculum of classical education with its seven liberal arts circumscribing learning and its dialectical method, to the much more flexible curriculum of modern universities where factual investigation has led to the admission of new kinds of knowledge both for research and teaching.

One clear sign of this change from a "single system of truth, anchored in God, and elaborated by man in accordance with a rigorous system of inference," was an antagonism to the "spirit of system" and an acceptance of the "separation of reason from faith, of philosophy from theology, and of logical and epistemological inquiry from ontological considerations."[24] If truth is not to be found in a system deduced from principles through syllogistic logic, but from facts induced from experimentation and analysis, then the wholeness of the medieval model was thrown in question. The self-evident unity of knowledge could no longer be assumed, and men became increasingly reluctant to commit themselves to any all-encompassing world-view.

What is considered universally self-evident now is what man can know and prove with his rational and empirical methods. Mastery of truth rests no longer in one's ability to prove by logic that something either agrees or disagrees with the principles of Aristotelian metaphysics or its Thomistic counterpart, but in one's "competence to isolate a problem, to exclude from view enough of the important, but not immediately relevant, data in order that one may study the problem by itself, and thus find for it a workable solution."[25] Hence it is interest in the part, instead of the whole, and acceptance of specialized truth, rather than total explanations, which characterize secular man.

> Secularized man selects a portion of reality in which he becomes an expert. He tends less and less to ask about the relation of this portion to the whole. . . . He tends to devote his knowledge or ability to the pursuit of limited and fairly immediate goals. To him the solving of problems, whether in human relations, in social and economic organization or in the mastery of nature, is a sufficient purpose and justification to his life and understanding. And secular man, at the highest levels of his self-consciousness, is a relativist but is not naive about the subtle temptations which beset him to absolutize his position. He is methodologically self-critical and seeks to refer all large ideas back to

the data of his science or the direct experience of his life. . . . He is
tempted on the one side by a complacent optimism about the world and
on the other by existential despair. But he tries nevertheless to live
and think in a relative, secular way.[26]

While others may not look with quite the same confidence
upon man's ability to live without some inclusive system of
thought, this is the posture which is required of men of faith
in the world. Gogarten grants that man cannot live without
faith in some unquestioned meaning, without a sense of ultimate wholeness and unity. Yet what man must forever seek
because of his creatureliness can only be received from God,
never achieved or produced by his own efforts. This does not
preclude a quest for insight and knowledge about the world, of
which science is the most notable example, but faith that ultimate
wholeness comes only from God insists upon the relativity and
partialness of all human findings, and objects when the part is
treated as the whole or when eternal truths are abstracted from
temporal events. Bonhoeffer had the same suspicion of total
explanations and "the will to ground" which seeks security in
fixed world-pictures or closed systems of truth.

Another mark of this transformation in man's attitude toward
truth is the change in the status of reason. The secularization
of knowledge, Gogarten observed, means that "ideas and knowledge which were previously considered revelation and mediated
acts of God and therefore accessible only to the faithful were
changed . . . into knowledge which is accessible to the reason
out of its own secular power, entirely unaided by faith."[27] This
can be observed in the growing autonomy of the various disciplines and their emancipation from the domination of medieval
theology, in the liberation of philosophy from its servant role
in relation to theology, and in the changing status of theology
in education.

Walter Moberly has traced the position of theology from its
virtual *monopoly* in the Dark Ages, when "the student learned
Latin in order to read his breviary, Mathematics to play his
part in managing the finances of the great ecclesiastical corporations, Logic and Rhetoric to expound Christian doctrine effec-

tively and to draw the correct conclusions from it, Music to understand the rules of plainsong"; through its *primacy* in the Middle Ages as "the queen of the sciences"; and its *equality* with the other disciplines in the latter part of the nineteenth century; to the present stage, with its *"bare toleration"* of theology. "Thus to-day the older struggle for supremacy has given place to a struggle for existence," Moberly concludes.[28] Inasmuch as theology always involves rational thought about divine revelation, the movement described here reflects the changing status of reason vis-à-vis faith. Yet insofar as theology is closely related to ecclesiastical authority and theological education is equated today with professional training for the clergy, its declining place in education may be a more apt reflection of the de-clericalization of education.

How is the heightened respect for human reason to be understood theologically? Both Gogarten and Bonhoeffer contend that the doctrine of justification by faith "secularizes reason" by liberating it from subservience to theology or the possibility of threatening faith. Faith does this on the one hand by exposing reason's soteriological efforts, any claim that it saves people because it possesses or reveals ultimate reality and wholeness; on the other hand by "remaining faith," resisting all temptations to invade those areas of life which have long since been turned over to the direction of human reason. Where reason violates its limits and claims to comprehend the world not only in its parts but in its wholeness, thus giving up its "questioning ignorance" and explaining away all mystery with an all-encompassing world-view, it both destroys the sense of mystery which is always part of human life and sacrifices its relative autonomy. Thus reason assumes an absolute autonomy which turns into a demand to be responsible for the wholeness and meaning of the world in addition to its particular order. As is always the case in the process of secularization, the resulting status ascribed to reason easily leads to such forms of secularism as pragmatism, operationalism, psychologism, relativism, and functionalism. For secular man is always tempted

to import a metaphysics which is unaware of its own character, masquerading as "science" or "reason" and therefore absolutizing a par-

ticular way of secular thinking; or to discount and dismiss all experiences of reality which escape the particular tools of perception
which a given secular observer uses; or to reduce man and his destiny
to an instrument of the technological process. . . . in all of these . . .
betraying his own relativity, pragmatism, and openness to reality.[29]

By "strengthening his secularity," the Christian faith both frees
man from the necessity for achieving ultimate meaning through
his own devices, through reason, and clarifies and protects the
relative autonomy of reason within the worldly order.

If human reason is "the organ of knowledge of the natural . . .
itself a part of this preserved form of life," then it is through
man's reason that he perceives what is natural as it presents
itself to him. As long as the natural realm is seen as penultimate
in relation to the ultimate, reason can function within it in "relative autonomy." "Relative autonomy" means "refraining from
taking the non-self-evident as self-evident,"[30] refusing to impose
any world-view as absolute upon science or social life. Hence, it
is not man himself but reason which in this view is autonomous.
The confusion of the autonomy of reason with the autonomy of
man leads to a new heteronomy of reason, whereas the proper
use of the legitimately autonomous reason becomes possible in
the light of faith.

The other phrase used in this connection was Bonhoeffer's
plea for "intellectual honesty," keeping human thinking "in
agreement with reality." It was in the name of "intellectual
honesty" that he bemoaned the continuing use of God as a
functional concept or substitute for rational explanation, and
the tendency to construct a system of general religious answers
to particular, historical world problems.

The process which has led to the emancipation of reason
from substantialistic metaphysical foundations and the removal
of disciplines from the supervision of theology is thus viewed
not as sinful presumption on man's part, but rather as part of
God's intention to be to man not a functional concept or working
hypothesis but a presence in the midst of life. It is God's intention that faith should be to man not a causal explanation or
otherworldly escape from responsibility but a call to responsible
involvement in the structures of the world.

In other words, in addition to denoting a radical alteration in man's understanding of the world, secularization theologically understood also includes the change in which truth is conceived in less substantialistic, static terms and in much more dramatic, active terms. It is a process in which only that which man can perceive and prove by his natural abilities is acknowledged as having self-evident, universal validity. It is a movement in which reason has been freed from the necessity for proving or agreeing with existing theological systems or religious traditions and has been granted "relative autonomy." But it is also a process in which liberated and autonomous reason constantly tends to absolutize its findings and offer its insights about the part as explanations for the whole.

This process has been encouraged by the concern to understand and be responsible for the world and by a reemphasis upon justification through faith, which relieves man from having to discover or develop ultimate truth or meaning through his reason, while providing reason with new freedom and responsibility within its particular relative realm. Wherever truth is seen in active, dramatic terms consistent with the historic character of human existence, and wherever the substantialist categories of classical metaphysics are considered inadequate to do justice to the existential quality of truth and persons do not insist upon the finality of existing knowledge—there secularization, thus conceived, has occurred. Wherever faith is turned into an all-encompassing world-view which provides eternal truths, or reason claims final authority, seeking to take the place of faith by providing ultimate meaning—there the process of secularization has been hindered by a faith which does not truly secularize reason, or by a reason which does not recognize its true relationship to faith.

Secularization as the Development of Historical Consciousness

The third transformation which the term "secularization" symbolizes is the development of Western man's awareness of the historicity of human existence. This development is illumined by the juxtaposition of the following descriptions of the Greek and modern attitudes toward history.

In its materialist and idealist moods alike, Greek thought tended to explain away both the outward appearance of physical things and the inward drama of personal life, and to see behind them no more than the cosmic or merely logical interplay of timeless and impersonal realities. At worst the mutable is mere illusion, at best a distant echo or unsuccessful imitation of the immutable. . . . in the Greek conception of history there is no room for the personal and purposive providence of the Bible. History, in the classical view, is endowed with shape but not with direction. It moves, like the planets, in perpetual cyclic revolution, an endless wheel of recurrence.[31]

In sharp contrast is this description of modern historical consciousness:

History . . . is not a description of events occurring on the surface of a world not history. History *is* a world, a *Lebenswelt*, a world of its own, the world it shapes. This world is not a neutral field existing outside men. It is the field of force they help comprise. . . . [Man] is in [this world] not as something to which he belongs but as something which belongs to him and for which he is responsible. History becomes a world only through the mediation of man.[32]

Although most historians might disagree with this picture of what it means for man to think of himself as historical, a number of writers have described the rise of historical consciousness in similar terms. Nicolas Berdyaev, for example, described the shift from a "static ontologism," a "metaphysical naturalism, which regards spirit as nature and substance" and subordinates history to nature, to a "historiosophy," a "metaphysic of freedom" which sees nature as a part of history, for "in history the destiny and meaning of world life is brought to light."[33] For Berdyaev this was the gradual triumph of the world viewed as history, anthropocentric thought, over the world viewed as nature, cosmocentric thought, in which Immanuel Kant was the pivotal figure.

Other writers have described man's growing awareness of himself as no longer timeless essence but as "a genuinely personal and historical being."[34] Whereas before, what was expected was single-minded acceptance of natural fate or speculation about the will of God and divine Providence, present historical consciousness emphasizes man's responsibility through decision and will.

To the widely accepted awareness that "what is not historical is for modern man not real," Gogarten adds his claim that this historical consciousness is the result of certain Christian insights and thus an aspect of secularization which the Christian faith seeks to preserve and encourage. Basic to any historical awareness is the biblical doctrine of creation, the conviction that God is the Creator who reveals himself through his act of creation. To speak of God means therefore to speak of his actions in man's behalf. To see the world as God's creation is to see it as a world of order and purpose which is expressed through human activity.

The belief that God involves himself in history in a unique way in Jesus Christ in the incarnation heightens interest in concrete historical events, in the particular as a source of meaning. As Bonhoeffer observed, the incarnation is a historical event which focuses all subsequent attention upon God not as a "supreme Being, absolute in power and goodness," but "God in human form . . . existing for others."[35]

The Christian understanding of man's responsibility for himself and for his world underlies certain presuppositions of modern historiography, such as the recognition of the difference and discontinuity between natural occurrences and historical human actions, the concern for the *meaning* of history over its "sheer factuality," the importance of human freedom which distinguishes history from nature, and descriptions of man as self-determining or self-constituting. Thus man's historicity is not simply the realization that he is historically conditioned, his sense of the timefulness of all things, nor is it his "sense of anachronism."[36] Rather, man's historicity involves his awareness of responsibility for his existence and for the world. Being a self becomes a responsibility rather than a given fact as human existence is viewed as a process of self-actualization and history is viewed as problematic.

The eschatological dimension of biblical faith contributed to man's historical consciousness not only a sense of direction, the notion that history is "going somewhere" and is not simply a natural cycle, but also an openness to the future and a sense of expectancy. Thus whereas medieval man considered reality as what was, is, and will always be, modern man tends to think of the real as "what is yet to be, what will come into being through him."[37]

Yet if the roots of the modern historical consciousness are to be found in biblical faith, the question posed previously must again be raised. Why the protracted interval between the time when Christian thought encountered European philosophy and the rise of historical consciousness? How can we account for the tardiness of the emergence of a science of history? Apparently, man's responsibility for the world, which is his historicity, was obscured in the dualistic thought of the substantialistic metaphysics of the Middle Ages. Hence it was only after the recovery of certain Pauline insights in the Reformation—in Luther's stress upon responsible sonship, filial freedom, and the importance of the secular disciplines—and the emergence of a genuinely Christian view of human existence that the science of history and the historical-critical method could emerge.[38]

Although Gogarten's explanation is far from satisfying, it makes clear his understanding of historical thinking and his reluctance to view history as a process within a stationary world or a sequence of events to be "explained" by clearly distinguished causal factors. In this kind of description of the way man understands himself in relation to history at particular times, Gogarten is vulnerable to the criticisms of those who claim he is playing fast and loose with historical data and projecting his own idealistic view of history. But in depicting secularization as historicization, contemporary theologians are engaged in putative prediction, seeking to provoke a new understanding of the nature of human existence and the demands of the Christian faith, rather than developing a Christian historiography.

The short-circuiting or perversion of the process of secularization viewed this way takes place when historical thought no longer remains open, when the eschatological dimension is lost, or when this openness turns into historical relativism or historicism which often leads to nihilism, or into historical scepticism which leads to "sceptical paralysis, pragmatic make-believe, or ideological fanaticism."[39] Or again it may turn into a progressivism which secularizes the eschatological understanding of history and turns it into a belief in rational progress or unlimited human perfectability. To keep history from being either supernaturalized or naturalized, Christians must protest against the "flight of modern historical thought into metaphysics" which offers universal laws or general interpretations of the actual course of historical events. Such "philosophies of history" can only result in an abandonment of history, in an evasion of the particular, Gogarten warns in terms reminiscent of Kierkegaard.

Such a historical consciousness also rejects any subject-object viewing of history, which destroys the character of the object, "history," by viewing it as isolated facts and thus denies man's involvement in worldly history, or destroys the character of the subject, "man," by viewing him as an isolated subject who must himself provide any meaning which history might have. By recognizing his secular responsibility, the Christian preserves his freedom to choose himself and the awareness that he is not self-constituted but can discover the true meaning of his existence only in encounters with others in the structures of the world.

In summary, the process of secularization involves the development of historical consciousness, seen not simply as a different way of viewing history but also as a radically different way of understanding human existence. This emerging historical consciousness is characterized by a distinction between nature and history, between natural events and human actions, a concern for historical meaning over objective factualness, an awareness that man is not the victim or slave of history, but responsible for it, and an openness to the future. Thus wherever there is genuine inquiry after meaning and not simply accumulation or chronicling of facts, wherever persons think of themselves as no longer at the mercy of fate or mysterious forces but as responsible for their life and its structures, and wherever history is seen as a mode of man's self-knowledge, not abstract data about the past—there secularization has taken place.

Wherever man is thought to be completely determined either biologically or environmentally, or human nature is thought to be fixed and man has no true freedom of "self-choice"; wherever history is viewed as nothing more than objective factualness, a sedimentation of events, which persons are to unearth and record—there the awareness of the genuine historicity of human existence has yet to develop, or has become separated from its Christian sources and perverted into some form of secularism. The Christian faith, however, seeks to maintain the true secularity of history by insisting that any unity or wholeness it has comes from God and that no human effort to supply a unified philosophy of history can provide an ultimately satisfying interpretation of its meaning.

Secularization
as the Decline of Ecclesiastical Hegemony

In his historical survey of the usage of the term "secularization," H. H. Walz shows how the term coined by a French envoy in the negotiations preceding the Peace of Westphalia (1646) slowly took on negative and polemical connotations as it began to be used to designate not only separation from ecclesiastical control but also independence of and hostility toward any form of religious domination.[40] This is the fourth substantial change included in the theological discussion of secularization, that is, the separation of properties, institutions, social services, and ideas from the control or guardianship of religious institutions.

Whether depicted as "mature sonship" or freedom from tutelage or childlike dependence upon religious hypotheses or ecclesiastical guardianship, the process described is one in which human institutions and individual persons are no longer dependent upon the authority of the church for their direction but are granted relative autonomy. In neither Gogarten nor Bonhoeffer is this process conceived to mean the withering away of the institutional churches but rather the development of a new relationship to ecclesiastical control which places upon persons the responsibility for seeking the meaning of their Christian existence in the secular world and for resisting any efforts to exert religious control over secular institutions.

Observers have variously described this process as Christianity's loss of influence in the arts, science, schools, and press, and in the consciousness of public life in general; as the substitution for church civilization of ideals "independently arrived at, the authority of which depends on their inherent and immediate capacity to produce conviction";[41] and as the development of pluralism "after a particular faith has been displaced from its monopolistic hold on culture."[42] It has also been described as the "shift of responsibility from religious authority to world authority," which resulted from the collapse of the medieval world-view. "Secularization came about with the recognition that the ordering of life fell to mankind under God and not by delegation from the religious hierarchy. Secularization represents the collapse of ecclesiastical totalitarianism."[43]

The decline of ecclesiastical hegemony is difficult to trace, however, for whereas the evidence of positive authority is clear enough—e.g., regulations, prohibitions, censures, censorship, or overt acts of persecution—the rejection of authority and corresponding loss of ecclesiastical influence is difficult to assess except in an impressionistic way. Nevertheless, it can be observed in such legislation as the repeal in 1871 of the English Subscription Law, requiring all candidates for university degrees at Oxford and Cambridge to affirm the Thirty-Nine Articles of the Anglican Church, and the passage of the Morrill Land Grant Act in America in 1862, establishing state colleges independent of church control or support.

Man's "derived independence," which motivates him to assume responsibility for the worldly order by making his own decisions and using his own reason, implies that he is no longer under religious surveillance. It means, for example, granting science "the right to an autonomous responsibility for its activity, unlimited by such alien laws as the faith of the church posed for it."[44] This independence from churchly control is rooted for Gogarten in the Reformation view of justification by faith, which distinguishes between the roles of saving faith and human reason, and in the Reformers' repudiation of "the medieval church's claim to sovereignty over the world and its orders."[45] Faith seeks to preserve the secularity of the various worldly orders by surrendering the world to man for his administration. According to Gogarten, the right of the church to control all human institutions was thrown into question by the gradual acceptance of an understanding of faith which makes it possible for persons to encounter God without the mediation of worldly institutions and by the realization that the Christian faith truly frees man for the kind of independence in which he must answer for himself before God.

In this sense secularization and Christian tradition are not in opposition. By emphasizing God's final prerogative in regard to man's salvation, the Reformation made possible a new freedom in relation to churchly tradition, throwing into question the equation of observable religious practices and the assurance of salvation.

The decline of ecclesiastical control began initially as a result of a misunderstanding of Luther's doctrine of the two realms, according to Bonhoeffer. Though intended as the emancipation and sanctification of the world, this was interpreted to mean the separation of law, economics, politics, and philosophy from their traditional theological bases. Yet in a Christocentric understanding of reality, man is responsible for preserving the relative autonomy of the various worldly institutions—not subjecting secular institutions to an alien rule, but freeing them to "attain to their own true character and become subject to their own innate law, which is theirs according to the manner of their creation."[46] The church's concern thus is not to reestablish its domination or to subject the secular institutions to ecclesiastical control but to set them free for genuine worldly service. The church is not to withdraw from the world into some "religious realm," but to proclaim the Word of God which calls men to true humanness and the world to genuine worldliness, protesting against any attempt to deify the world or to "re-religionize" man.

In the late Paul Tillich's understanding of the theonomous function of faith, the secular institutions are viewed as dependent upon God for their ultimate meaning, but are independent and autonomous in relation to ecclesiastical institutions. Conversely, this implies that the function of the church in relation to the "secular" is not one of domination or even secret lordship, but one of ministry and service.[47]

Protestantism demands a radical laicism, Tillich contended, for it not only questions the absolute authority of any religious institution and repudiates the classical distinction between sacred and secular spheres, but also overcomes the gap between priesthood and laity. As the medieval tendency to see education as a monopoly of the clergy broke down and the new lay educated class developed, an independent ideal of lay culture arose, so that universal education, laicism, and anticlericalism became interrelated in the process of secularization.

> . . . there is no doubt that the progress of universal education has coincided with the secularization of modern culture and has been very largely responsible for it . . . While the clergy studied the Bible and the Fathers, the laity studied the classics; while the clergy studied the history of the Church, the laity studied the history of the State; while the clergy studied the traditional Christian philosophy, the laity studied the philosophers of pagan antiquity and the new natural sciences. . . . when we remember how for the last four hundred years the sphere of lay education has been steadily widening, and that of clerical education has been narrowing, it is difficult to exaggerate the effects of this division on the secularization of modern civilization.[48]

One other theological explanation for the church's decreasing authority in the political and educational realms can be traced back to Pope Gregory IX's insistence that "just as the Triune God has the three attributes of *potentia, sapientia,* and *benignitas,* so the three orders of society, though they be one in Christ, should enjoy a measure of autonomy."[49] This led to a distinction between the unique and independent functions of state, university, and church which Harvard historian George Williams has traced through Alexander of Roes, the medieval University of Paris, Calvin's Genevan Academy, and Cambridge University, to the Harvard of Increase and Cotton Mather. This distinction underlies what is today called "'critical pluralism'— the constitutional preservation of centers of relative autonomy in order to secure Christian society from aberrations in the name of piety or patriotism."[50] Williams ably demonstrates the persistent influence of this theological motif and the contribution it made to secularization because of the relative autonomy which the church eventually accorded both the state and the university, more often by necessity than choice.

Thus the process of secularization becomes perverted where the source of freedom is not recognized; where the dimension of faith is denied; where persons seek their own salvation and that of the whole world by setting up some earthly factor, idea, nation, race, or political theory as the highest value to which all else is subordinated; or where the relativity of all earthly things is not recognized in relation to the ultimate. Or it is short-circuited when the church tries frantically to dominate the decision-making of persons who have reached maturity.

Secularization understood as the development of a new relationship to religious authority and ecclesiastical control has eventuated in countless forms of secularism. On the one hand, the secular element absolutizes its autonomy and establishes a realm of its own, putting reason in place of faith in a debased form of rationalism which does not recognize any other sources of truth and claims that reason is capable of providing man's ultimate meaning and salvation. In like manner, totalitarianisms absolutize particular ideologies and claim autonomy from the basic reality of God and hegemony over all other worldly structures. On the other hand, under the threat of reason's increasing power, theologians often turn faith into a competing world-view, making improper claims for faith. Fighting for the preservation of the church's authority, churchmen seek to extend ecclesiastical domination by imposing certain demands in regard to the state, science, and education, or by extolling the superiority of their religious explanations over those emerging from the secular disciplines.

> Secularism in religion is the substitution of religious structures and authorities for the Gospel. . . . the attempt to preserve a fragment of absolute authority for the churches in a secularized world, denying man's responsibility for his future and making faith secondary to institutional loyalty. . . . The churches, in this state of secularism, call men away from historical responsibility to an ahistorical, unchanging truth.

Secularism in contemporary Christianity is also expressed as clericalism. . . . the attempt to project the role of the clergy in the old Christendom into the era of a secular world. Thus, ordained leaders of the churches preempt the responsibility of the laity, treating responsibility in the world as essentially nonreligious, while the activities of the religious institutions are viewed as *the religious works.*

Whether secularism appears as absolutizing a religious dogma or preserving a fragment of official authority or segregating a special sphere of life from the rule of faith, in every case the historical task of man as decision for God in history is denied and another authority is substituted for the sovereign Lord of history.[51]

In summary, a fourth change denoted by the term "secularization" is the decline of the churches' imposed authority, the rejection of ecclesiastical control, and the assumption of relative autonomy by institutions and individuals. It is a process analogous to personal growth, through conception and nursing, guardianship and tutelage, to self-conscious independence and autonomy and, hopefully, responsible sonship. When autonomy has been absolutized, secularization has resulted in a bondage to worldly absolutisms, and the resulting secularism usurps freedom and imposes a new bondage. When the autonomy has been withheld or denied in the interest of prolonged childhood, secularization has been prevented by a clericalism which understands neither the nature of Christian freedom nor the meaning of true humanness and genuine worldliness.

Wherever institutions founded by the church and church-supported have been turned over to state or alodial bodies and granted relative autonomy; wherever religious authorities have relinquished their dominant or controlling relationship to public institutions, de-confessionalizing them and freeing them from all repressive coercion, while reminding them of their special responsibility within the world; wherever persons have accepted responsibility to seek the meaning of their existence within the autonomous structures of the world without deifying the world or absolutizing these structures; wherever persons are seeking to make decisions in the world in accordance with the Christocentric view of reality which seeks the fulfillment of the allotted functions of the orders of creation—there secularization has occurred. But wherever a penultimate realm claims absolute authority, cutting itself off from other realms or subordinating them to it; wherever the clergy seek to establish control over secular structures or to maintain tutelage over persons who have the freedom and ability to make their own decisions; or wherever the churches so absolutize their own activities and loyalties as to divert persons from responsible participation in secular institutions—there the process of secularization has either been perverted into an "erroneous worldliness" or into "clerical secularism." Hence the maturity of a secular institution will be reflected in the way it relates to the structures of religious authority, accepting their servanthood role without submitting to the church's externally imposed control. And the maturity of the churches will be reflected in the way they relate to secular institutions, respecting their autonomy and helping them fulfill their purposes, insisting all the while that such institutions never deprive individuals within them of those decisions wherein they encounter the concrete reality of God in the world.

Secularization is herein defined as that historical process within Western thought in which man has undergone a radical transformation in his understanding of the nature of the world, truth, history, and religious authority. As long as the Christian roots of these insights, man's responsibility for the world, and the possibility of ultimate wholeness and meaning are recognized, secularization remains a creative process in which man discovers what it means to be truly human. But when the derivedness or relativity of human existence is denied or man seeks to dissolve the tension by all-inclusive or religious world-views, then secularism results and man forfeits his freedom and puts himself in bondage to a "spurious worldliness" or inhuman religiosity.

CHAPTER 4

The Secularization of Higher Education in America

To see if the concept of secularization provides a suggestive way of reassessing the development of American higher education, it is necessary to re-view certain basic changes which have occurred in university life to see how they are illumined by the use of this theological symbol. Such a sharpening of focus is justified by the recognition that universities are microcosms, reflecting the changes in thought in the culture at large, and by the widespread designation of American higher education as "secularized." Since most American colleges were founded by churchmen and were concerned with the perpetuation of a "religious culture" up until the Civil War[1] but today are considered "secular" in orientation and purpose, it is clear that some radical alteration has taken place, a change usually labeled "the secularization of higher education."

Yet, whereas this phrase has traditionally been used by churchmen in a pejorative way and been narrowly conceived as the triumph of materialistic values over spiritual values,[2] the theological use of the term rehearsed above suggests a far more profound meaning. Using the term "secularization," therefore, to denote the radical reorientation in Western man's understanding of himself in relation to the world, truth, history, and religious institutions, this theological assessment of culture provides a way to re-view what has happened in the last three centuries and suggests an attitude toward secularization which protests against any resolution of its dialectic tension into a closed ideology, into secularism.

Without rehearsing in great detail the history of American higher education, it is possible to come to a deeper understanding of its development by focusing upon four basic changes which reflect its secularization. Only after examining this descriptive use of the term—as denotation of the development of experimentation and research, the expansion of the curriculum, the increase in faculty and student freedom and responsibility, and the declining hegemony of the churches in higher education—will it be appropriate to turn to its normative implications.[3]

The Rise of Experimentation and Research

The contrast between Plato's disdain for factual research, reflected in his suggestion that the works of Democritus, the great Greek physical philosopher, be burned, and the modern university's reverence for scholarly research suggests the incredible development of investigation and research in higher education. While it is not historically accurate to belittle the scientific concerns of the early Greeks or to overlook the Aristotelian combination of factual and conceptual research which flourished in the Alexandrian School (306 B.C.–A.D. 642), it appears that factual investigation was eclipsed by conceptual analysis until the Renaissance of the fourteenth and later centuries. So, although the medieval teachers were indeed investigators, they limited their investigations to verbal knowledge and rationalistic debates, organizing into a conception or theory facts already in hand or postulated as collectible, and showing little interest in experimentation or factual investigation. Their role was simply to conserve and master that which was.

With the work of Kepler (1571-1630), Galileo (1564-1642), and Francis Bacon (1561-1626) there arose a new concern for demonstrable efficient explanations which began to threaten the preoccupation with speculative teleological explanations. This took place, however, largely outside the universities, leading to the founding of the scientific societies.[4] The aversion of the English universities to the methods and findings of the "new science" has been explained by Arnold Nash as follows:

> Experiment to the Schoolmen was unnecessary: man knew the truth, for example, about falling bodies; his only concern was to work out the

implications of what he already knew. The stars, being heavenly bodies, were known to be perfect, hence to look at them was a waste of time. Any direct frontal attack on this intellectual self-satisfaction was bound to fail.[5]

Thus the advocates of scientific training and research were under suspicion until the last of the nineteenth century and were frequently considered godless by those who considered the universities to be nurseries of the church. Only the Dissenting Academies in England reflected agreement with the scientists on the need to reorganize the curriculum so as to overthrow Aristotle and make possible an espousal of the Baconian point of view.

> For the most part Oxford and Cambridge continued to be universities in the tradition of a Christian interpretation of the Graeco-Roman classics till the latter part of the nineteenth century. . . . This was the "idea of a university" which Newman loved so much.[6]

Exceptions to the hostility toward the "new science" were the universities of Utrecht and Leyden, where the influence of the more radical, Calvinist wing of the Reformation accounted for their willingness to reorganize their systems in a way comparable to the Dissenting Academies.

With the introduction of experimental science at the Pietist-controlled University of Halle in 1694, German universities began to respond to the demand that academic communities take seriously the world as a realm to be studied, explored, and explained. The founding of the University of Berlin in 1809 marked the culmination of a revolution in German university life.

> The scholastic philosophy of Aristotle was superseded by a more modern philosophy founded upon the principles of the physical sciences and mathematics; the hard-and-fast curriculum was replaced by one embodying the principle of freedom of research and instruction; mere exposition of a canonical text was replaced by the systematic lecture; the disputation was replaced by the seminar; a sound and vital classical scholarship replaced the formal imitation of the classics; and, finally, the German language ousted the Latin as the medium of instruction.[7]

In the United States, Harvard adopted with little change the curriculum of Cambridge, a "proper amalgam of the medieval arts and sciences and of Renaissance interest in the study of literature and belles-lettres."[8] Yet apparently by 1659 the Ptolemaic system was dead at Harvard and the Copernican system fully established. With the arrival of Charles Morton, a leading teacher from one of the English Dissenting Academies, Harvard's course in natural philosophy took on a decidedly Newtonian orientation.[9] The appointment of Isaac Greenwood as the first Hollis professor of mathematics and natural philosophy in 1727 marked the triumph of Newtonian science and a new attitude toward "practical" subjects.

But Harvard was not alone in making such appointments. In 1711 the College of William and Mary named a Mr. LeFevre as professor of natural philosophy and mathematics. Provost William Smith of the University of Pennsylvania succeeded in instituting a program (between 1740 and 1800) in which approximately forty percent of the classroom time was devoted to scientific studies.[10] And by 1792 botany was being taught at Columbia, and in 1795 John MacLean at Princeton became the "first professor of chemistry in an American college."[11]

The influence of these early professors cannot be overestimated in the secularization of American higher education. As Hofstadter notes,

> In all the colleges the first professor of mathematics and natural philosophy was the first professor of a secular subject. Often he was also the first professor whose personal background was secular. While an able professor of science was like an able professor of divinity in the sense that he had something distinctive to bring to the college, something besides mere conformity, he was different in that he introduced the *discovery* of knowledge into the classroom.[12]

Nevertheless, the presence of professors teaching mathematics and natural philosophy (the earliest name for "science" in American colleges) and the addition of scientific studies to the curriculum did not automatically produce a burgeoning of scientific research. With a few notable exceptions, "instruction was didactic and catechetical . . . Scientific speculation was diverted either to natural theology, where the conceptual framework was given, or to survey, classification, and invention, where the conceptual content was slight."[13] Even where there were flourishing scientific schools, like Lawrence at Harvard, Sheffield at Yale, and Chandler at Dartmouth, they functioned separately from the main structures of the colleges.

The founding of Johns Hopkins University in 1876 marked a turning point, however, in the acceptance of experimentation and research, giving American higher education not only the clearest copy yet of German graduate scholarship, but creating a new confidence in research. By 1899, President James P. Angell of the University of Michigan could boast that "the method of scientific instruction has been revolutionized. In the last half century no more important step in education has been taken than in the universal introduction of the laboratory methods."[14]

Without filling in additional details of the development of experimentation and research in American higher education in this century, it is enough to note one writer's listing of the basic assumptions which now undergird university life to indicate how far it has come in accepting the demand to extend the areas of knowledge through factual research. These assumptions are commonly accepted:

> (a) that the universe is inherently worth studying; (b) that the material world is not evil, and that we need not fear what our researches may disclose; (c) that nature is orderly; (d) that Truth is one, and that ultimately there can be no conflict between what is known to be true in one sphere and what is known to be true in another; (e) that the human reason is a sound means of acquiring knowledge and ascertaining the truth; (f) that there is a relationship between cause and effect, and that therefore the experiments of one person may be tested, and either confirmed or refuted, by the experiments of another; (g) that the experimental method is itself satisfactory as a basis for establishing any hypothesis; (h) that in any conflict between them ideas must be subordinated to facts; (i) that ignorance is dangerous, and that there is a duty to discover and make known the truth; (j) that antiquity does not of itself accord validity to ideas, however venerable they may seem to be.[15]

The theological insights detailed above suggest that these assumptions are integral to the Christian faith, arising from the biblical understanding that the world is neither evil nor sacred, but man's inheritance and responsibility, to be studied, explained, and utilized. They also reflect a growing distrust of religious answers which use God as a "stop-gap" for human ignorance or seek to point man away from the need to seek meaning in penultimate forms. In this sense, the development of experimentation and research in the universities can be seen as part of man's response to the changed view of the world described above. Opposition to this development arises most often from those who still regard the world as sacred or those whose obscurantist versions of the Christian faith have been so systematized as closed world-views that the discovery of new truth about the world seems threatening to them.

This religious opposition was late appearing in America, since the earliest professors of natural philosophy were deeply religious men who viewed science as a tool to demonstrate the wondrous ways of God. Besides, as already noted, the Puritan acceptance of "intra-mundane interests and thorough-going empiricism" created an atmosphere of ready acceptance of new discoveries concerning the physical universe. But as the authority of science increased, it presented not only a "special conception of truth and a formula for tolerating error" but a threat to the hegemony of received theology and the authority of the clergy.

Hence by 1700, conflicts between faith and scientific rationalism began to appear, arising in part because of the unorthodox views of certain scientists, and in part because science was perceived as a threat to the preeminence of the clergy. Conflicts between sectarian interests and the scientific spirit increased following the Civil War with the increasing acceptance of Darwinian thought, a conflict which one writer observes was "less a matter of whether evolution was true than a matter of whether the old regime or the new regime would prevail, whether piety or intellect, whether authority resting on received truth or on scientific evidence."[16] " . . . science and education joined forces to attack two major objectives—the authority of the clergy and the principles of doctrinal moralism—and . . . one of the effects of this coalition was the hastening of academic reform."[17]

Thus the rise of science—with its ethical neutrality, pref-

erence for experiment, and indifference to inherited truth—
gradually undercut the "doctrinal moralism" of the colleges,
the assumption that "character was a function of belief," which
equated a professor's academic competence with his orthodoxy
and excluded religious nonconformists, and the assumption that
"an idea was warranted and verified by proof of its moral
advantages," which rejected any theories that might have "im-
pious and harmful consequences."[18]

Equally important in accounting for the growing recognition
of the research function was what Walter Metzger calls the
shift from "conserving" to "searching" in the American university faculties after the Civil War.

Acceptance of the unfettered search for truth which underlies experimentation and research not only flourished but soon
began to dominate American higher education, provoking a
protest from those who felt that the blind aping of the German
scientific spirit soon becomes dehumanizing and "servile,"[19]
and that overemphasis upon scientific research often leads to
indoctrination into a "naturalistic faith." More recently has come
the protest against the apparent victory of empiricism in American universities, that brand of positivism which calls "positive"
only those things and facts of immediate perception and exalts
"science as the only valid method of acquiring knowledge and
understanding."[20] Such positivism often leads to "intellectual
obscurantism" because of the limitations it places upon truth,
confining the search for knowledge to the empirical method and
meaning to rational intelligibility. The success of man's "conquest of nature," which has given him a sense of mastery in a
realm where meaning can be equated with rational intelligibility, especially with rational, analyzable, natural, and efficient
causes, has prompted this reductionism and its subsequent
denial of the historic dimension of human life and the banishment of mystery from the realm of meaning.

In the present context, scientism, positivism, empiricism, and
naturalism are to be understood as forms of secularism, fruits
of the human concern to understand the world and examine it
in a scientific way, which, denying the world's derivedness or

their own relativities, claim to provide a total, and therefore exclusive, explanation for human existence. The current emphasis upon research accomplishments over instructional capacity in American universities, the prevailing imperialism of empiricism in the social sciences, and the "intellectual obscurantism" of those who deny theology any place in the curriculum or refuse awe and wonder a place in the university ethos—all come from the same historic impulse, i.e., the university's desire to provide a structure for the conservation and extension of human knowledge. This is an effort strengthened by secularization but perverted when the ultimate wholeness and meaning which come only from God are claimed by any ideology.

The Expansion and Revision of the Curriculum

A second basic change in American higher education illumined by the theological understanding of secularization is the revision of the curriculum. In oversimplified terms, this is that battle-fraught movement from the religious-classical prescribed curriculum of the Old American Literary Colleges, through the rise of the elective principle, to the development of general education in its various forms. The numerous social and historical factors involved, the conflicting philosophies of education invoked, and the dependence upon certain charismatic presidents and professors make this movement a difficult one to chronicle.

Nevertheless, the changing understanding of truth reflected here and the active role played by churchmen both in encouraging and resisting curricular reform suggest that the shift from the restricted course offerings at early Harvard to the vast programs available today represents not only a quantitative difference, a "knowledge explosion," but also the kind of radical reorientation in human thought symbolized by the term "secularization." Hence this change requires treatment in a theological consideration of secularization.

The historical roots of the seven liberal arts, which formed the basis of the curriculums of the first American colleges, may be traced to the second century B.C. when the Roman scholar

Varro sought to establish in Rome a system of education based upon the Greeks', including nine liberal arts: grammar, rhetoric, logic, astronomy, arithmetic, geometry, music, architecture, and medicine. This number was reduced to seven by Martianus Capella in the fourth century A.D.—the *trivium* of grammar, rhetoric, and logic, and the *quadrivium* of arithmetic, geometry, astronomy, and music—keeping "only those arts which would interest a group of celestial beings," and omitting medicine "because celestial beings had no earthly ills" and architecture "because spirits needed no physical habitation."[21] Capella's predisposition for spiritual rather than material things helps explain how the vast Greek intellectual heritage became condensed into the seven liberal arts, a tradition officially accepted by the church fathers as the minimum training for prospective priests and teachers. Because training in the liberal arts was required preparation for theological study, the church felt it necessary, in order to prevent the rise and spread of heresy, to control all entrances into the teaching profession, granting a license to teach only upon the completion of the liberal arts course; thus began the practice of the prescribed curriculum.[22]

After the rediscovery of Aristotle's "New Logic" in the twelfth century, his three philosophies—natural (physics), moral (ethics and politics), and mental (metaphysics)—were added to the seven liberal arts to make up the medieval arts course. Renaissance additions to the prescribed curriculums of the medieval universities brought a new humanistic interest in the Greek and Roman classics and marked the beginning of the substitution of the authority of classical antiquity for the authority of the church. Emphasis upon the work of the individual typified the early Renaissance, prompting this definition of the liberal arts from Peter Paul Vergerius during that period:

> We call those studies liberal which are worthy of a free man; those studies by which we attain and practise virtue and wisdom; that education which calls forth, trains and develops those highest gifts of body and of mind which ennoble men, and which are rightly judged to rank next in dignity to virtue only.[23]

This concept of liberal education was "on the whole, *secular,* deep-rooted in this-worldly concerns and aims. . . . *aristocratic*, redolent of the ideals and standards of a ruling class. . . . [and] *uncommitted* to anything beyond an amorphous humanism as an explanation of the meaning of existence."[24] Erasmus and others led the movement to include classical Greek and Latin in the curriculum and Petrus Ramus in France sought to reform the liberal arts by making them more applicable to social use and freeing them from ecclesiastical control. Trinity College, Cambridge, was founded in 1546 with regius professorships in Greek, Hebrew, and civil law, marking the transition from medieval to humanistic studies.

Early Protestantism embraced this Renaissance humanism, stressing the value of the study of classical languages for biblical studies and literary understanding and the Reformers' conviction that education is not under the control of special revelation but falls within the province of common grace and hence is equally accessible to Christians and non-Christians. Roland Frye writes in his monograph on "Protestantism and Education,"

> . . . at whatever point I have examined the first century Protestant practice it appears to have been a matter of adopting and implementing Renaissance educational ideals. Except in the extreme sects, these educational ideals seem nowhere to have been opposed and everywhere to have been advanced. So firmly established did they become that the classical curriculum of Oxford and Cambridge . . . remained essentially unchanged from the sixteenth century to the nineteenth century.[25]

Yet all too soon the Renaissance's new learning, which had "broken through a petrified medieval tradition to bring new enthusiasm, relevance, and vitality to education," itself hardened into a scholastic mold, leading newer humanists like John Milton to protest, as had Erasmus earlier, against this new "stultification of learning." In spite of the major innovations being introduced into the curriculums of the Dissenting Academies—the study of English and French language and literature, modern history, and experimental science—at Oxford and Cambridge the new humanism was "essentially digested into the continuing scholasticism . . . and the virtual idolatry of the ancients which persisted for generations."[26] This explains, in part, the content of Harvard's early curriculum, modeled as it was upon the gentleman's education of Cambridge, and coming as it did "after the new learning of the renaissance had been sifted into the old scholastic curriculum, but before the new scientific leaven had begun to work."[27]

Thus the original prescribed curriculum of the American colleges was the product of the merging of (1) the medieval idea of the necessity of the seven arts for a liberal education and preparation for further professional study in law, theology, and medicine; (2) the Renaissance ideal of the study of the classics as the basis for a liberal and "gentlemanly" education; and (3) the Reformation stress upon higher education as necessary for the training of leaders in church and state,[28] which led to the founding of most of the nine pre-Revolution colleges.

Although there were scattered efforts at revision, there was no substantial curriculum change in the American colleges until 1825 when the University of Virginia opened with eight separate "schools," independent of one another, teaching the ancient languages, modern languages, mathematics, natural philosophy, natural history, medicine, moral philosophy, and the law, and with students free to choose the school within which they would study. That same year, in response to the influence of the German universities, Harvard divided instruction into various departments and began to allow students to select their studies. Faculty opposition made this change short-lived, but this provided impetus to curricular reform elsewhere.

In the meantime, the Yale Report of 1828 presented a classic defense of the prescribed curriculum which was to be used repeatedly as a weapon against any substantial change.[29] Drawing heavily upon the widely held "faculty psychology" of that time, which believed that the mind consists of discrete faculties or powers like attention, imagination, judgment, and memory, the report stated:

> The two great points to be gained in intellectual culture, are the *discipline* and the *furniture* of the mind; expanding its powers, and storing it with knowledge. . . . A commanding object, therefore, in a collegiate course, should be, to call into daily and vigorous exercise the faculties of the student.[30]

But the proliferation of new knowledge in the nineteenth century so deluged the world that the fixed curriculum envisioned by the Yale faculty in 1828 was soon swamped by such overlapping waves as technological knowledge (engineering and agriculture, which were either taught in parallel courses for special students or dominated such schools as Rensselaer Polytechnic Institute and Michigan State College), modern language and literature (notably French and German), experimental science, the social sciences, philosophy, and the fine arts.[31]

The passage of the Morrill Federal Land Grant Act in 1862 represented one response to this deluge. Based upon Congressman Morrill's suggestion that American colleges might well "lop off a portion of the studies established centuries ago as the mark of European scholarship and replace the vacancy—if it is a vacancy—by those of a less antique and more practical value," the Act provided for the establishment in every state of at least one college "where the leading object shall be, without excluding other scientific or classical studies, to teach such branches of learning as are related to agriculture and the mechanic arts."[32]

With the election of Charles W. Eliot to the presidency of Harvard in 1869, American higher education had a leader responsive to the flood of new learning. Rejecting the earlier "faculty psychology," Eliot introduced an elective system to make the new knowledge available to all who wanted it, "a device for bringing a new spirit of inquiry and scholarship into the life of the university and for bringing Harvard itself once again into a position of commanding leadership in American life."[33] He began in 1872 by abolishing all subject requirements for seniors, and so succeeded in expanding the domain of election that by 1897 the prescribed course of study at Harvard had been reduced to a year of freshman rhetoric.

Needless to say, the response to Eliot's reforms at Harvard was mixed, supported on the one hand by men like Andrew D. White of Cornell, William B. Rogers of M.I.T., Daniel C. Gilman of Johns Hopkins, David S. Jordon of Stanford, William

R. Harper of Chicago, and Frederick A. P. Barnard of Columbia, but strongly opposed by men like Noah Porter of Yale, Franklin Carter of Williams, Alexander Winchell of Syracuse, Asa D. Smith of Dartmouth, and James McCosh of Princeton.

In spite of all efforts to preserve the prescribed classical curriculum, by 1901, according to a survey of ninety-seven representative colleges, thirty-four were offering courses of study which were seventy percent elective, and twelve were offering programs over fifty percent elective.[34] Most responsive to the elective principle were the large state universities of the Midwest and West; least responsive were those in the South and the small colleges of New England.

> In the end, [the elective principle] was the instrument, secular and democratic, that permitted the American university to enter into a vital partnership with the society of which it was a part. It transformed the English college in America by grafting upon it German ideals and in the process created the American university.[35]

Although the motives for supporting or opposing revision of the curriculum were mixed, and limited finances or controversial personalities often abetted institutional opposition to change, it is possible to list several general convictions which prompted or delayed the reform. Behind the expansion were the following reasons: (1) a conception of the dynamic nature of truth which refused to accept as adequate or definitive a curriculum drawn up centuries before, and which insisted upon the need to recognize and include the specialized knowledge streaming from European universities and scientific academies; (2) a conviction that a self-evident source of intellectual unity could no longer be found either in theology or its Renaissance synthesis with classical tradition, but must be sought elsewhere or dispensed with; (3) a revised conception of what constitutes an educated man, emphasizing functional as well as traditional cultural studies; (4) a confidence in the ability of students to choose in a mature way when granted freedom, stressing learning over character formation as the purpose of education; (5) an enlarged notion of who should be educated, so that education might serve not simply as preparation for the professions or training in "polite learning," but as a universally liberating force in society available to all who desired it; and (6) a recognition of individual differences in interests and abilities which necessitated diversity in course offerings and rejected the "faculty psychology" which prompted the teaching of the same courses to train the same faculties in every person.

The reasons cited for opposing curricular reform were these: (1) a continuing confidence in the adequacy of the classical liberal arts course and a conviction that anything else would not be liberating; (2) a conviction that specialized or professional education should be carried on only after, and separate from, liberal education; (3) a lack of confidence in the ability of students to choose wisely from varied course offerings or to profit from college life without strict supervision; (4) a strong belief in "faculty psychology" and its insistence that the mental discipline required for the study of the ancient classics was far more conducive to learning than the freedom and initiative demanded by the sciences; (5) the belief that indoctrination in revealed religion can best be provided within a prescribed curriculum in which one studies the "ancient God-given truths"; and (6) a fear that the growing emphasis upon the practical and the individual in higher education would lead to an infinite proliferation of courses and undisciplined chaos in the elective curriculum.

In "the exuberance of freedom," the elective principle was soon carried to such extremes as to fulfill the worst fears of its critics, providing indiscriminate sampling of courses by students, destroying any sense of coherence or unity in the curriculum, and greatly overloading catalogues, faculties, and budgets in a harried effort to "give students what they wanted" rather than what the classical educators felt they needed. "Freedom for the student to choose became freedom for the professor to invent; and the professor's love of specialization [became] the students' hate of fragmentation. A kind of bizarre version of academic laissez-faire" emerged.[36]

The reactions were loud and varied. Irving Babbitt and the "New Humanists" attacked the notion that universities should simply disseminate practical knowledge, contending that education was becoming dominated by scientific materialism and a preoccupation with power, "a humanitarian substitution of service of man for the service of God."[37] From a different perspective, Abraham Flexner castigated the loss of any definite aim, any unity of spirit or purpose in American higher education, insisting that "in the reckless effort to expand, and thus to cater to various demands, the university as an organic whole has disintegrated."[38]

John Dewey and the progressive educators reacted against the compartmentalization and depersonalization of the expanding elective system by suggesting that students be prepared to meet novel situations by an education which is training in problem-solving. Alexander Meiklejohn, José Ortega y Gasset, and others called for a radical curbing of course offerings. But most influential, perhaps, was Robert M. Hutchins' protest against empiricism, vocationalism, and pragmatism in American higher education. He advocated a forthright return to the scholastic curriculum, to "the single-minded pursuit of the intellectual virtues," a "general education in the classics, grammar, rhetoric, logic, and mathematics, all to be ordered through the guiding influence of Aristotelian metaphysics."[39]

So widespread was the reaction to excessive curricular expansion that almost every institution began limiting its electives in some way, either by instituting a distributive principle, adopting a system of "concentration" or "majoring," or developing comprehensive survey or core courses to balance the emphasis upon specialization. Based upon the need to recover some communality and unity in the undergraduate learning process, the general education movement began at Columbia in 1919 with integration courses in Contemporary Civilization (Social Science), the Sciences, and the Humanities required of all freshmen and sophomores. This movement was adopted at the University of Chicago in 1931 and came to fruition at Harvard in 1945, following the publication of the Harvard Report on *General Education in a Free Society.*

The need for some organizing principle or source of intellectual unity, how to relate general and specialized education in such a way that the latter does not overwhelm or under-privilege the former, the need to insure adequate instruction in the humanities, and the confusion concerning the purposes of higher education—these are some of the problems which still haunt educators in the wake of the radical curricular re-visions rehearsed above and the counterrevolution which followed them.

One other dimension of this development which should be noted is the displacement of the study of religion from college curriculums during the secularization of American higher edu-cation.[40] Harvard's historian Samuel Morison repeatedly em-phasized "the ideal of learning through Christ . . . attaining a more perfect knowledge of God by the discipline of the mind, [which] dominated Harvard College at least until the American Revolution."[41] Daily readings from the Hebrew Bible required of the freshman class and studies in divinity, i.e., the catechetical, biblical, and scientific study of theology, equipped any Harvard graduate to interpret the Bible accord-ing to acceptable hermeneutical studies and to discuss the ma-jor theological issues of his day.

The Yale curriculum of 1828 reflected the same combination of classical arts and Christian theology, with required courses in Bible, the biblical languages, moral philosophy, natural theol-ogy, and the evidences of Christianity (apologetics). With the exception of William and Mary, where the Chair of Divinity was abolished in 1779, almost every existent college, including the earliest state schools, provided instruction in religion before the Civil War, usually culminating in a required senior course in moral philosophy and Christian Evidences taught by the president, which provided "a rationally defensible and impreg-nable *Weltanschauung* by which to live."[42] One manifestation of curricular transformation was the gradual deletion of re-ligion courses, particularly after the Civil War.

At least four different factors contributed to the decline of course offerings in religion. The first was the protectionist concern of orthodox churchmen in relation to heterodoxy, which

provoked criticism of religious instruction and led to the establishment of separate, denominational seminaries, e.g., Andover
Theological Seminary—which was founded in 1808 by the de-
fenders of orthodox Calvinism after the confirmation of Uni-
tarian Henry Ware as Hollis Professor of Divinity at Harvard—
and Princeton Seminary, which was established in 1812 by
Presbyterians no longer satisfied with the orthodoxy of Princeton
College.[43] Thus began the unfortunate split between liberal
education and theological studies and the establishment of denominational seminaries apart from universities, which led to
the theological deprivation of the liberal arts and the pro-
fessionalization and isolation of theology, as well as to the
widely held notion that the study of theology is of value only
for the clergy.[44]

Closely related to this was the accentuation of the denominational spirit in America beginning in the late eighteenth
century and on into the nineteenth century which prompted the
equation of theology with narrow sectarianism and the assumption that there could be no teaching of religion which was not
sectarian, ergo divisive. This encouraged the popular belief
that the doctrine of the separation of church and state requires
the banishment of all formal teaching of religion from state-
supported schools.

A third factor contributing to the extrusion of religion was
the developing critical and scientific spirit which was suspicious
of traditional apologetics, that is, arguments from miracle, de-
sign, or analogy between nature and Scripture, and which raised
serious questions about the soundness of the "unscientific" theological method for arriving at truth about religion. And fourthly,
two centuries of immigration, mostly Roman Catholic and Jewish, radically altered the Protestant character of the American
population. The concern for voluntaryism and pluralism which
arose out of an increasingly heterogeneous populace hastened
the decline of the Protestant establishment and threw into question the teaching of any theology not acceptable to all persons.

As a result of these various forces, by the first part of this
century only the church-related colleges and a few private

and state-supported institutions offered any full systematic instruction in religion, with such courses as existed being offered in the English or philosophy departments ("The Literature of the Bible" or "Philosophy of Religion"), in semi-independent and denominationally staffed "Bible Chairs," or in separate schools of religion. With the modification of the elective system and the reaffirmation of concern for liberal education in the last two decades, however, there has been renewed interest in the inclusion of the scholarly study of religion in university curriculums, reflected in the establishment of many new departments of religion, an overhauling of existing religion courses, and a genuine effort to relate religion to the total liberal arts program.[45]

What light does the theological understanding of secularization shed upon this process of curricular revision? Clearly the historical development reflects a revision in the content of education, from relatively fixed courses which fit a free man for oratorical or political skills (early Roman), or prepared one to study theology, law, or medicine (Middle Ages), or fit men "for publick Imployment, both in Church & Civil State" (Yale's charter), to any training which helps one fulfill his responsibility to be human in today's world. This is a shift from education which subjectively liberates man from ignorance and prejudice to that which also equips him to contribute to the upkeep and ordering of the world, his inheritance. It reflects an understanding of truth which is not static or fixed, to be recovered or uncovered from the past, but truth which is dynamic and functional, to be discovered and proved in every new age by means accessible to all. In a day when specialization focuses interest upon the part and away from the whole or total explanation, it reflects a view of knowledge which is ever expanding, whose unity is no longer self-evident. And it reflects a changed view of theology, from that all-pervasive *Weltanschauung* which "holds all things together" and permeates all studies, to a limited subject taught to potential clergymen as preparation for the professional ministry.

Contributing to this development, according to this theological perspective, was the biblical concern that man assume dominion over the created world. Equally important was the Reformation recovery of the Pauline understanding of justification by faith, which frees man from the need to earn his salvation either by good works or right reasoning, and "secularizes" human reason by freeing it from subservience to revelation or ecclesiastical authority, thus ascribing it a "derived autonomy" in the penultimate realms. Such a change occurred as the Christian faith ceased to be threatened by expanding knowledge, abdicated its role as world-view, and prompted in men a "questioning ignorance" toward the world which accepted no curriculum as final and no method as absolute.

It occurred as scientific theories rendered unnecessary a functional use of God as an explanation and encouraged in men that intellectual honesty which keeps their thinking in agreement with reality and prevents them from using religious answers as substitutes for knowledge or as escapes from responsible involvement in the world. Where the functions of faith and knowledge were confused, and where new knowledge was regarded as a threat to faith, an erosion of biblical truth, or a usurpation of the traditional "evidences of Christianity"—there the religious forces opposed the inclusion of new learning.

Viewed this way, one reason for the gradual exclusion of courses in religion from college curriculums may have been the failure to distinguish between the teaching of religion and the practice of religion, between efforts to explore and attempts to convert. As the self-evident validity of the Christian faith as a world-view and the need for a God of explanation to fill the gaps in human knowledge declined, so the interest in religion courses in apologetics, based upon clerical or administrative authority or arguments from the evidences, declined; or put more accurately, so the suspicion of the inclusion of such courses in the curriculum of state and private institutions increased. In any case, as long as theology felt itself in the position of having to oppose new learning, it tended to respond in a doctrinaire fashion or to sacrifice its distinctive contribution and follow a path of increasing capitulation until it no longer occupied a significant place in the college curriculum.

The excessive freedom of the elective principle and its sacrifice of any order in the curriculum, the triumph of functional education and utilitarian professional training over "liberal" or liberating education, the extrusion of courses in religion from the curriculum of many universities—all are evidences of the same perversion of the secularization process observed before, producing the various forms of secularism already noted: pragmatism, operationalism, and utilitarianism.

The Increase of Faculty and Student Freedom and Responsibility

A third change in American higher education is the movement from early domination by trustees and presidents to the present division of responsibility, the result of increased faculty and student participation in policy determination. Although many persons today long for an earlier time when, they erroneously assume, the lines of authority were clear and teachers simply taught, students studied, and presidents and trustees "administered" the colleges, the numerous recent efforts to analyze the power structure in American higher education suggest that its future rests in large part upon clarification of the meaning of academic freedom and who is to control the universities.

According to Hastings Rashdall's classic study of the medieval universities, during the first three centuries of their development the Italian schools were student controlled.[46] The students, usually studying law or medicine, hence older than today's undergraduates, hired and fired teachers, formulated rules for governing the schools, and chose the towns where they were to be located. When controversies arose with local authorities, the students moved elsewhere, relocating the universities. For the universities were wherever the students were. But because of frequent disputes over housing and disorderly conduct—the earliest "town-gown" conflicts—by the fifteenth century municipal authorities began to take over and govern the Italian universities at Salerno, Bologna, and Padua. As the lay bodies of nonacademic people assumed the governing power in these early universities, the professors became hired employees. Thus began the pattern of academic government which can be traced through the Italian-influenced University of Leyden to the Scottish universities, and thence to the United States.[47] In Paris, on the other hand, the university chartered by the king in 1200 was under the control of a guild of masters from the outset. There, because of the need for decent housing and inexpensive board near the lecture halls, masters, who were also clerics, began to provide accommodations for the poorer students, thus establishing in the thirteenth century the first residential colleges. As these colleges became better established and endowed and the authority of the masters increased, student powers, previously vested in student "nations," declined.

Transported to Oxford and Cambridge, this college pattern soon replaced the existing university structures, with its stress upon communal living and "cultural" training to prepare men for service in church and state. In the colleges, beginning with Merton at Oxford in 1264, masters provided a liberal education for "gentlemen at large." The roots of Harvard's collegiate structure can be traced to Magdalen College (Oxford) where undergraduates paid for the privilege of being boarders, receiving, in return, most of their instruction from college lecturers. This led, as it had at Paris, to a change in student discipline and "autocracies administered by masters." As the colleges assumed responsibility for the moral and physical as well as the intellectual life of students, the concept of "collegiate life" emerged whose aim was "the formation of a pure and manly character."

Harvard, a virtual copy of an English college, duplicated not only its classical literary curriculum but also its concern to maintain discipline and cultivate the "collegiate way of living" (Cotton Mather). But for various reasons, primarily financial, the earliest college buildings in America were not built like the quadrangles of the English colleges, and it was far more difficult for the tutors at Harvard to maintain control and detect disorder than for the dons at Cambridge. Thus inexperienced and ineffectual supervision produced friction which infected the teaching relationship and led to strict regulations based upon a parental theory of discipline. The frequent student riots and abuse of professors and tutors in the early American colleges attest the student resentment of this paternal discipline and regimentation.

Under the libertarian influence of Thomas Jefferson, a new attitude toward student responsibility was evidenced at William and Mary in 1779 with the first real attempt at student government. But a subsequent effort at the University of Virginia in 1825, also under Jefferson's influence, was "quickly abandoned . . . when all the professors tendered their resignations."[48] Student involvement in college administration throughout most of the nineteenth century was restricted to a few successful experiments at Oberlin, Antioch, and Amherst, as two conflicting theories of education sought acceptance. Most prevalent was the emphasis upon tradition in the antebellum colleges, which supported a paternalistic authoritarianism and discouraged participation or self-expression by students, who were regarded as "morally deficient or immature" as well as "intellectually innocent and impressionable."[49]

In contrast to the earliest colleges' acceptance of responsibility for the whole life of their students—housing, personal counsel, social supervision, vocational guidance, and character training—was the German pattern with its emphasis upon intellectualism. If man is a purely rational creature, capable of controlling all his actions, as the Enlightenment spokesmen claimed, then a university's sole concern is with the minds of students; it has little interest in where or how they live, eat, or worship. The Reformation's destruction of the celibate and cloistered life of the German universities, with their old ecclesiastical order, and the location of general education in the secondary schools had already ended any emphasis upon communal college life in Germany and considerably raised the age of its university students.

With the founding of the University of Berlin in 1809, the concepts of *Lehrfreiheit* and *Lernfreiheit,* the essential ingredients of German university life, attained their fullest expression. By *Lehrfreiheit,* the German professor meant his freedom to examine bodies of evidence and report findings in lectures or publications, that is, freedom of teaching and research. But it also implied a minimum of administrative regulations within the teaching situation, that is, freedom from tutorial duties, prescribed syllabuses, and a fixed curriculum. And by *Lernfreiheit*, German educators meant "the absence of administrative coercions in the learning situation," the freedom of students to move from place to place, to determine the choice and sequence of their courses, to attend class when they wished, and to live in private quarters and control their own lives.[50] Without these twin freedoms, according to the Germans, no institution could claim to be a university.

So along with the influence of the Germans upon the curriculum came the claim that university education required some of the same freedom for American students and faculty. Wayland at Brown, Tappan at the University of Michigan, and eventually Eliot at Harvard began to echo these ideas, indicating that they meant the end of the traditional disciplinary function of the college and decreased responsibility for the private lives of students, a position under much discussion in the press throughout the latter part of the nineteenth century.

While these two points of view were vying for dominance in academic circles, students themselves were reacting to the increasing paternalism of the traditionalists, the mounting impersonalization of the intellectualists, and the seeming irrelevancy of the prescribed curriculum by developing their own extracurricular activities.[51] Student debating societies, residential fraternities, intercollegiate athletics, and college newspapers developed and spread following the Civil War as students found more creative forms than riots to protest their disenchantment with the collegiate discipline, resentment of their German-influenced professors' preoccupation with research, and disaffection for the prescribed curriculum. The power of the extracurriculum rapidly increased to the point where it began to overwhelm the curriculum, however, prompting on the one hand reforms to make the curriculum more interesting (e.g., first Eliot's electives and then Lowell's "concentration" program at Harvard), and on the other hand efforts to curtail the extracurriculum (e.g., Hutchins' reforms at the University of Chicago).

At the same time there emerged a renewed emphasis upon the "education of the whole man" which affirmed the importance of extracurricular activities (now called "co-curricular") as integral to the learning experience, a reassertion of the wholistic view on the basis of a quite different psychology of learning, stressing the development of personality rather than the disciplining of the faculties of the mind.

In the last three decades, student involvement in policy-making through student government structures, as well as participation in some instances in admissions, promotions, and long-range policy decisions, indicates a growing acceptance of the notion that students should have a role in determining the future of higher education. If the riots at the University of California at Berkeley are any indication, this requires more than the "strictly academic influence" which students inevitably exert as "consumers" through their choice of courses or their patronage of particular teachers.[52]

Two strands emerge out of this tangled web of developments. One is a mounting demand for fuller participation by students in shaping university life, viewed not simply, as above, as a means for heightening the individual student's maturity, but based upon a conviction that students have a valuable and necessary contribution to make to higher education. This reflects the prevailing view that the educational experience is one in which students must participate actively to benefit. The other is a growing discontent with the paternalistic forms in which universities have traditionally expressed concern for student life which questions the notion that the college should function *in loco parentis*. This reflects not only the heightened development of individualism in morality, a "privatism" which marks the current reorientation in morals, but also a growing division between the academic-institutional demands of the college and the private life of students. Widespread student demonstrations, beginning with the monumental jurisdictional dispute at the University of California at Berkeley, indicate that the major questions here remain unresolved in many universities, e.g., what part students should have in policy determination and what role the institutions should play in supervising student life. There seems to be general agreement that higher education requires some order in the legal, social, and moral realms; but much less agreement as to the most creative balance of individual freedom and institutional responsibility and the place of administrative authority.

The changing role of faculty in American higher education somewhat parallels the changing role of students just described. Influenced more by the Scottish than by the faculty-controlled English universities in developing administrative structures, the early American colleges were governed by nonresident boards of trustees, who in turn employed the president and faculty. This structure has remained virtually unchanged, although the control of the boards shifted out of the hands of the clergy and into the hands of lawyers and businessmen in the nineteenth century. From the outset, the president—often referred to as the "head professor"—sat on these external governing boards, but not the professors, who initially were considered too young and too transient to govern.

During the early years the professors were "intellectual generalists" who taught a variety of courses, assisted with administration and discipline, and filled a pastoral or character-developing function in the communal colleges. But with the rise of the natural sciences, the development of research, and the influence of the German pattern of impersonalism in faculty-student relations, the professors' function changed to that of imparting technical and compartmentalized information. Increasing departmentalization and specialization and the rise of professional societies and identification with a particular discipline decreased institutional loyalty and involvement of faculty in administrative decisions. At the same time, the increasing size of institutions and the complexity of administrative decision-making turned the college presidency into a job requiring special competence, no longer to be performed by a leading professor.

Hofstadter and Metzger have described the hazardous relations of professors to nonprofessional boards of trustees and dictatorial presidents, concluding in their studies of academic freedom in the United States that the unique set of problems posed by the ambiguous status of American professors in the university organization accounts for the tendency to discuss academic freedom in institutional rather than educational terms.[53] Thus, shortly after their selective importation, the German concepts of *Lehrfreiheit* and *Lernfreiheit* became separated in American higher education, with the main emphasis upon professorial freedoms, "producer rather than consumer freedom." This is reflected in the earliest statement of the American Association of University Professors on Academic Freedom and Tenure, in 1915, which noted at the outset: "It need scarcely be pointed out that the freedom which is the subject of this report is that of the teacher."[54]

In addition to clarifying their academic freedom (usually focused in problems of dismissal and tenure), faculty also exercised authority in the areas of admission, curriculum, examinations, class schedules, and the granting of degrees. Yet even here, administrative vice-presidents, deans, and ancillary non-teaching personnel now make many of the decisions formerly in the hands of faculty. There has been, of course, active faculty participation in the formation of university reforms, e.g., the Yale Report of 1828 and the Harvard Report of 1945 were both the work of faculty committees. But the faculties of American colleges have usually had little control over the institutions where they teach.

This sense of impotence regarding actual policy determination may help to explain the rapid growth of the American Association of University Professors and the various professional societies, as well as the tendency of faculty to side and identify with student demands for greater freedom and more responsibility. In any event, although great strides have been made in securing and protecting academic freedom, the status of the faculty in the "city state of the university" (Kerr) at times seems no clearer than that of students, as the location of real power in higher education moves outside the community of scholars and students and into the hands of research-supporting foundations or government agencies, budget-granting legislators and politicians, or support-granting alumni and general public. Noting that increasing pressure will also be exerted on colleges and universities by the communities surrounding them, one observer predicts "no foreseeable end to the vitally important struggle to win or defend freedom [to learn and teach] where it means the most—right at the grass roots of every campus in the land."[55]

Viewed from the theological perspective explicated above, this increasing demand for faculty and student participation in the shaping of higher education is consistent with the biblical understanding of the importance of human freedom and responsibility. Just as the mysterious fatefulness of the natural order was overcome by the recognition that the world is "just world" and dependent upon human effort for its upkeep and "penultimate meanings," so the awesome givenness of the university world was diminished by the recognition that the educational process and the structure of the curriculum are dependent upon the decisions of responsible persons. In this sense, the development of a historical consciousness, defined not simply as "a sense of history" or concern for the past but as responsibility for shaping the future, can be seen reflected in the growing demands of faculty and students for participation in the determination of higher education. Refusing to view the past as rigidly determining or the future as decided, such a stance accepts responsibility for shaping the present in the concrete situations of daily existence. Insofar as both faculty and students became uneasy about the restrictive atmosphere which determined them and began to demand freedom to choose and shape their own life within the university, they seemed to become aware that the university, as their world, is not simply something they belong to or are located in, but something which belongs to them and for which they are in part responsible. Thus, they may be said to have accepted their historicity by demanding responsibility for their world and freedom to participate in its formation.

This movement reflects, too, an understanding of freedom

which insists that in some sense one must be free *from* the confining regulations which keep him feeling childlike before he can be free *for* the kinds of decisions which lead to adulthood. As long as education was considered primarily character-development and students were treated as completely immature and incapable of making basic decisions for themselves, and faculty dared not deviate from a fixed syllabus or single interpretation of truth, there could scarcely be much sense of responsibility among faculty or students. Today, the removal of many early restrictions upon faculty and the willingness to entrust students with more self-determination than ever before are indicative of a willingness to recognize their potential maturity and to treat them as persons accountable because they have been made free from petty restraints and free for responsible action. Although structures and regulations are always necessary in an educational institution, and one phase of the process of becoming mature involves learning to live creatively within such structures, the present mood also reflects the conviction that learning to handle freedom and to make decisions in a social context is one phase of the process of becoming truly human which should be available in the college experience.

The movement also reflects the view of truth suggested above in which learning involves not simply hearing and repeating objective facts, but inquiring after meaning, seeking purpose and direction through participation in the learning process. Describing the characteristics of our present age, in which responsibility and freedom are the root-metaphors, one professor has written:

> Becoming an adult no longer means fitting into a ready-made world order, accepting *what is,* but assuming the responsibility for creating those relations which will constitute the community. It is a new world, Teilhard de Chardin remarks, in which "as happens already, one gives one's life to be and to know, rather than to possess." These are the words that identify the twentieth century: creativity, responsibility, and community.[56]

Of course, this increased freedom of faculty and students is on occasion abused. Rebellion against rules and regulations has often produced antinomianism, on the one hand, and relativism which leads to nihilism, on the other, both absolutizing freedom and forgetting responsibility. The removal of all sanctions and structures of authority has also led to intellectual anarchy on occasion or the confusion and emotional fatigue which result from a purely nondirective, permissive approach to learning.[57]

Faculty and student demands for reform of existing regulations have at times been irresponsible, just as trustee efforts to preserve harmony and maintain a benevolent paternalism have at other times proved debilitating. In both instances, the result has often been antithetical to the purposes of the university, as victory, not truth, has become the aim; facts have been used as weapons to score on opponents rather than as instruments of enlightenment; and character assassination and simplistic theories of conspiracy have replaced respect for differences and awareness of ambiguity which characterize the academic community at its best. The moral absolutism of many campus reformers, faculty and student, has led to hopes for an instant millennium, just as simplistic demonology has led to the belief that the conquest of a few immediate obstacles would produce the longed-for new order on the campus, a perfect academic community.

The Decline of Denominational Control in Higher Education

Institutions of higher education are excellent illustrations of the process of secularization understood as the decline of religious authority or ecclesiastical control. America's first colleges, established with but few exceptions by committed churchmen on explicitly religious grounds, soon began to broaden their control and aim until eventually it became necessary to claim independence from all ecclesiastical authority. This change, like those described above, occurred not suddenly or decisively but over a period of a century and a half and in a host of small decisions. In some instances, it resulted in a deep appreciation for an institution's heritage but a repudiation of its parochial limitations. In other cases, the break occurred so completely that all vestiges of denominational sponsorship or religious inception were expunged and a self-conscious autonomy claimed. Hence the true secularity of an institution today is often reflected in the way it regards its religious roots.[58]

Perhaps the clearest index of the churches' declining influence on American higher education is the loss of explicit control of their educational institutions. In contrast to the medieval universities, where education was in the service and largely under the control of the Roman Catholic Church—which promulgated bulls authorizing universities, protected them against the state, and determined what books could be used and what ideas taught—and the English universities, which were chartered and protected by Parliament, governed by masters, but in fact were largely under the control of the Established Church, the American colonial colleges were founded by churchmen and chartered by the states, but were governed by nonacademic boards representing the public at large. Hofstadter calls this a pattern of "essentially private denominational sponsorship, with a modest admixture of state supervision."[59] As long as the population was homogeneous in religion, as in the theocracy of the Massachusetts Bay Colony, the control of the colleges, while not officially under ecclesiastical bodies, was in the hands of churchmen.

This was the "religious era" of American higher education. If no formal tests or oaths of conformity were required, comparable to the Subscription Act for Oxford and Cambridge, it was not because conformity was not expected, but because the religious homogeneity made such requests seem superfluous. Established primarily as "nurseries for ministers" and fostered as children of the established churches, these earliest colleges reflected the hopes of their founders to train men for active participation in church and state.

The concern to maintain orthodoxy played an important part in the establishment of the first colleges, e.g., Yale's founders were disturbed by the latitudinarianism appearing at Harvard, and, later, Amherst's Congregational founders objected to the Unitarianism appearing at Harvard. Even when the settled churches began to become austere, rigid, and removed, the inspired preaching during the "Great Awakening" produced a new concern for orthodoxy and renewed interest in colleges, leading to the founding, around the middle of the eighteenth century, of Princeton by the New Side Presbyterians, Brown by the Baptists, Rutgers by the Dutch Reformed, and Dartmouth by Congregationalist Eleazar Wheelock, with the motto *Vox clamantis in deserto*.[60] Not only these colonial colleges, but practically all the colleges founded between the Revolution and the Civil War were organized and in large part controlled and supported by religious interests.

With the disestablishment of the traditional churches after the Revolution, a new concept of the role of the state began to emerge. Interest in state-controlled institutions of higher learning led not only to the establishment, near the close of the eighteenth century, of public universities in North Carolina, Tennessee, Vermont, Georgia, and South Carolina, but also to the feeling that existing colleges should be made more responsive to the public will. Efforts to bring six of the nine colonial colleges more closely under state control were finally halted in 1819 by the Dartmouth College decision, after the New Hampshire legislature had sought to alter Dartmouth's charter. Since this decision forbade the interference with private and denominational colleges by the state or public, it encouraged the establishment of hundreds of new church colleges and in large measure checked the development of state universities until after the Civil War.

Coming as it did precisely when the "Second Awakening" was reaching its peak, this decision marked the beginning of the "denominational era," in which higher education in America was regarded primarily as the responsibility of the denominations. Not only did the old colleges of the East experience a new and fervid evangelical zeal, but the same concern which had led to the founding of Yale and Harvard, heightened now by the aggrandizement of sect, prompted the establishment of denominational schools throughout the country. Of their "church-relatedness" or sense of mission there was little question.

The few state universities founded during this era were

dominated by denominational interests. Even the University of Virginia, established as the epitome of secular and republican learning, was reshaped by the pressures of the state's denominational forces which succeeded, following Jefferson's death, in giving it "the character of a religious institution."[61]

But soon rising dissatisfaction with denominational dominance of higher education and a popular demand for institutions more directly responsive to the public will and needs of the day led to a renewal of the public education movement. Whereas previously it had been felt that the existence of many well-established church colleges made it unnecessary to spend huge sums for the operation of state colleges, the opinion began to spread that "the colleges established and fostered by the churches were not sufficiently broad in their outlook and sympathies."[62]

The event which marks the transition from the "denominational" to the present "secular" era in American higher education was the passage of the Morrill Land Grant Act in 1862, subtitled "An Act donating Public Lands to the several States and Territories which may provide Colleges for the Benefit of Agriculture and the Mechanic Arts." This act was important not only for what it did to the curriculum of American colleges, but also because it brought the government, on both state and federal levels, clearly into the support of higher education, and, by incorporating the equalitarian rationale of the Jacksonian era, made available popular higher education for the first time. Whereas the colonial colleges had existed primarily for the aristocracy and served as doors into the learned professions, the land-grant colleges opened up higher education to the middle and industrial classes. Thus was established the multiplicity, the mixed economy of American universities, which forms the basis for our present system of mass education.

Not only did the land-grant acts of 1862 and 1890 prompt the founding of new state colleges, sixty-nine of which are still in existence today, but they also encouraged the transfer of church colleges to state control, e.g., Alabama Polytechnic Institute, the University of California, Kansas State College, Colorado School of Mines, the University of Delaware, and the University of Kentucky. Thus colleges moved further away from denominational control as public funds became available and as administrations began to turn to business interests and foundations rather than to churches for support. The careful stipulation by Andrew Carnegie that benefits from the Teachers Insurance and Annuity Program of his Carnegie Foundation (chartered in 1906) should not be available to "sectarian institutions" also encouraged many denominational colleges to sever all official connections with their parent bodies. For whatever reasons, by the second decade of this century many institutions that were denominational in inception had moved to state or private control, a move described by some as "coming of age."

A second evidence of the diminishing influence of the churches in higher education is the disappearance of many of the religious practices which once characterized most colleges. Although agreement with the Westminster Confession and Saybrook Platform was apparently expected of the students and officials at Yale in 1748 and students at the University of North Carolina were forbidden to "deny the being of a God, or the divine authority of the Holy Scriptures" by the university laws of 1813, there seems to be no evidence of religious tests for faculty or students in American colleges.

Compulsory prayers and chapel services were almost universal symbols of religious concern in state as well as private schools, beginning to disappear or become voluntary only during the second half of the last century. Revivals were considered one of the most effective agencies of religion in college life before the Civil War, and most college presidents and faculties felt they had failed a collegiate generation if there were no rousing revivals during its four years.

But these "spontaneous" religious experiences of the early years were gradually replaced by the activities of the growing student religious societies which in turn were absorbed into the more inclusive and socially alert intercollegiate YMCA, beginning in 1857-1858 at Michigan and Virginia.[63] Because of their nonsectarian aims and service orientation, the Y's received preferential treatment by the colleges and were able to carry on student religious activities long after the colleges had ceased official sponsorship. As the emphasis upon the preparation of men for the ministry waned and the original curriculums were revised and expanded, required religion courses were deleted or made optional. Thus did the evidence of traditional religious control in American higher education disappear.

The decline of religious practices in the state institutions was not primarily or even largely in deference to constitutional mandates but, according to one authority on the legal aspects of higher education, is more accurately attributed to

> a growing secularization of society, the adoption of the elective system in institutions of higher learning, the unpopularity of chapel services with students, and the lessened intellectual respectability of religion as the result of the new sciences.[64]

The principle of separation of church and state had important implications for the early institutions, challenging the exclusive privileges of the Anglican colleges in Virginia and New York, and the Congregational colleges in Massachusetts, Connecticut, and New Hampshire; yet it has seldom been the reason for abandoning religious practices in higher education as it has in the public schools. The diminution of religious practices in state universities has been the result rather of changing constituencies in the states and heightened sensitivity to the implications of religious pluralism, as Protestant Christian baccalaureate services have been revised or abolished, university sponsorship of a single Student Christian Association has been withdrawn, and Religious Emphasis Weeks have been made tri-faith or abandoned.

A third, more subtle index of the displacement of the churches from university life is the laicization of higher education, that is, the disappearance of the clergy as an academic force. As long as one theological position or religious group dominated a community and there was little religious nonconformity, clergymen occupied a place of preeminence in colonial life. Hence the earliest college presidents and a majority of the trustees were clergymen, and the faculty, when not already ordained, were often tutors preparing for the ministry. Although the percentage of clergymen on the faculties began to decline by the end of the eighteenth century, the faculties of the liberal arts colleges before the Civil War remained largely clerical. After the war this clerical dominance sharply declined.

The laicization of the college presidency took longer to accomplish. Before the Civil War eleven out of twelve college presidents were clergymen. The nomination of John Leverett, a layman, to the presidency of Harvard in 1707 marked a departure from clerical administrations, prompting from Cotton Mather, who had hoped for the presidency himself, this protest:

> . . . to make a lawyer, and one who never affected the study of Divinity, a praesident for a College of Divines, will be a very preposterous thing, a thing without a precedent. [If the General Court would reject Leverett] . . . the Churches might yett be saved.[65]

But thanks to the machinations of Governor Dudley, Leverett was approved in 1708. Dartmouth was next with the election of John Wheelock in 1779, but with the exception of Columbia, William and Mary, and the University of South Carolina, which seemed more receptive to lay presidents, almost everywhere the presidency remained in the hands of clergymen. Cornell and Johns Hopkins began with lay presidents, but Princeton, Amherst, Brown, and Hamilton did not appoint laymen to the presidency until this century. This same tendency prevailed in the state universities, e.g., the University of Georgia continued the tradition of a clerical president for over a hundred years.[66]

Boards of trustees were also predominantly clerical in the early years, even in state institutions. But with the development of religious pluralism, the declining authority of the minister in American life, and the demand to include college alumni on the boards, clerical dominance declined. According to a study of fifteen private colleges, in 1860 clergymen made up 39.1 percent of their boards, whereas by 1900-1901 this had dropped to 23 percent and by 1930-1931 to 7.2 percent.[67] Symptomatic of this change were the twelve Baltimore citizens Johns Hopkins selected to establish his university in 1867: seven businessmen, four lawyers, and a doctor. Laymen were finally admitted to the

Yale Corporation in 1871 over the opposition of the controlling clergy.

A number of factors contributed to this declericalization of American higher education. It reflected in one sense the displacement of the church from its hegemony in colonial America, a reaction against the church's frequent claims to monopoly on truth, and a tendency to consider the church only one of several sources of guidance. It also reflected a disgust with denominational aggressiveness and sectarian bickering and a growing tolerance of various religious positions, the result of growing pluralism which led at times to intolerance of the spokesmen of any particular denomination. Voluntaryism undermined any remaining authoritarianism. It represented an impatience with the kind of clericalism which often sought to control the dominion of knowledge and to assert the superiority of religious explanations over all others. The doctrine of scientific competence tended to discount such presumed omniscience, to expose cultural obscurantism, and to circumscribe clerical authority, demanding of the man of knowledge "cultivation rather than consecration, accomplishments rather than observances, skill and method rather than piousness."[68] And the exchange of clerical for industrial patronage doubtless reflects the need of struggling colleges for financial support, political influence, and practical leadership which prompted a preference for businessmen, lawyers, and persons more skilled in the ways of the world than the clergymen of the age seemed to be.

Where secularization is conceived as the declining hegemony of the churches in higher education it can be understood theologically as a reflection of the growing self-consciousness and autonomy which communities of learning demand. Although most colleges were established by the churches in their concern for liberating and humanizing truth and the propagation of the Christian faith, the colleges have sought freedom from ecclesiastical as well as political control as they have developed an understanding of what is required of an autonomous community of learning, that is, not to be subject to an alien law but free to attain its own true character. Such colleges have demanded freedom from subscription, religious regulations, loyalty oaths, and external domination, insisting that *libertas christiana* includes freedom from doctrinaire loyalties as well as freedom to pursue the truth. And as church educational institutions have "come of age," and sought to exercise maturity and assert their independence, denominations have had to surrender or liberalize their control of these institutions, not depriving their trustees and faculties of responsible decisions but reminding them of what it means to decide and act responsibly. Thus the churches have moved from the domination of higher education to ministry and service within it.

As a result of the decline of the absolute authority of religious institutions, the eclipse of ecclesiastical totalitarianism, and the growing recognition of man's responsibility in the world for its structures, a radical laicism is beginning to emerge. This laicism, on the one hand, resents and rejects any form of clericalism— any attempt by clergymen to preempt the responsibilities of laymen or to exercise control over persons who can act maturely —and, on the other hand, remains open to the illumination of biblical faith in the exercise of responsible freedom.

Where universities have forgotten or denied their religious heritage and absolutized or idolized their autonomy, they have often sacrificed their derived freedom and become enslaved to some ideology, e.g., nationalism, empiricism, or liberal rationalism. Where colleges have remained under the close supervision of parent bodies, not exercising their freedom either to explore the truth or to act responsibly, independent of religious sponsorship, they have tended to be parochial, uncreative, and often defensive. Here sectarianism has produced a form of secularism which perverts the process of secularization and prevents the realization of genuine worldliness within the university.

Having reviewed the development of American higher education in terms of its secularization, it is possible to turn now in the final chapter to the normative implications of the concept, drawing upon the principles and themes suggested above for a formulation of the relation of the church to secular universities which will be both "appropriate to the Republic of Letters" and aware of the "critical pluralism" which characterizes secular higher education today.

CHAPTER 5

The Church and the Secular University

> The university, like the world, must find in the modern age, not a new intellectual synthesis to replace the one it lost in the Middle Ages, but a genuine openness to all aspects of the search for truth and the service of man. It must, in other words, remain secular, without a faith or philosophy of its own. Yet this secularity must have a certain character which it is the Christian's responsibility to help it to achieve.[1]

Although it has been pointed out repeatedly in recent years that there is no systematic and prescriptive Christian system of education, and the positing of one reflects a misunderstanding both of the nature of faith and of education, many writers have suggested ways in which biblical insights illumine the human problems that arise in education. For if education is, in fact, a human enterprise, not a religious one, and the Christian faith is concerned not with making men religious in an otherworldly way, but in calling them to responsible participation in the world, then the church's interest in higher education arises from its concern for "making and keeping human life human" (Paul Lehmann). In this sense, the church[2] looks at higher education not as a realm to be captured and exploited for religious purposes, i.e., to gain followers or to propagate certain doctrines, but as a matter of worldly concern equally accessible to Christians and non-Christians.

Although filled with clichés about "taking the university seriously" and "letting the university *be* the university," many discussions of the purpose of higher education by churchmen in the past two decades have tended to import from Christian theology a whole series of notions about how universities should be run, subjects taught, and truth unified. To those colleges which seemed hopelessly secularized (meaning in this case, separated from denominational control), the churches dispatched campus pastors, dedicated, as one of them put it, to "the restoration of God in education."[3] Such discussions and ministries have seemed, however, to draw upon some normative image from the past, failing to take seriously the radical dimensions of secularization in higher education and longing wistfully for a pre- or post-secular day.

After an examination of the reinterpretation of the concept of secularization and its implications for understanding what has occurred in Western thought, chapter 4 sought to explore what illumination a theological understanding of secularization might shed upon the development of American higher education. Insofar as this provoked new insights about the present situation, it validated the use of secularization as a descriptive concept.

Yet the normative implications of this concept are equally important. Hence, it is necessary also to inquire into the relation of the church and secular higher education suggested by this way of viewing intellectual history. If secularization is interpreted as a historical process of reorientation in man's understanding of the world, God, and himself, a process for which biblical insights are in large part responsible, then the task of the church in higher education is not to belittle its advent but to understand its roots and accept it, on the one hand, and to prevent its perversion into secularism, on the other. For this basically liberating development has been menaced whenever its necessary dialectical tension has been resolved and the resulting points of view made into closed systems.

The development of secularization in higher education is not to be deplored, therefore, but welcomed as an integral part of the process in which modern man has "come of age." Christians are called to full participation in the life of the secular university not because they want to infiltrate, restore, or dominate it, but because it is part of the created world, the inheritance turned over to them.

At the same time, this acceptance of the university as part of God's creation which is to be sustained is only half of the dialectical tension of faith which must be maintained. Along with this affirmation of the secularity of the university, i.e., its freedom from all externally imposed controls, is the demand to preserve its secularity from perversion. So a willingness to affirm the university is always accompanied by a demand to be critical of it, to protest against anything within its life which would subvert its freedom of inquiry, absolutize its relativity, or dehumanize its learning process.

> [The Church] must accept that the business of the university is the critical examination of everything. When it sees that absence in the university, when it sees indoctrination or the exclusion of certain valid concerns, the Church must protest, not because religion or Christianity is getting poor treatment, but because the educational task is neglected.[4]

Academic man's proclivity for total explanations which thwart or pervert the process of secularization has been observed repeatedly above, underscoring the difficulty in maintaining a "creative secularity" which affirms authentic worldliness and judges any spurious worldliness in which the world is no longer seen as derived and penultimate. Precisely because of their openness, universities contain within them many aprioristic systems which close themselves off from interaction with other positions. Against these and all ideologies which menace the openness and freedom secularization has made possible, protest must be raised. In four areas of university life this need for affirmation of secularity and judgment upon secularism can be illustrated.

Receptivity to All Forms of Truth

One of the chief characteristics of the process of secularization is a genuine openness to all forms of truth. This stems from the conviction that God as creator has turned over the world to man as his inheritance, and that man's responsible sonship requires understanding and ordering of the world of men and nature. Freedom from fear of a de-divinized world liberates one to investigate, control, and use it. The New Testament concept of sonship makes this investigational function not simply a possibility but a duty for one who would fulfill his humanity by accepting responsibility for the world.

By distinguishing clearly between the saving work of God

in Jesus Christ which makes possible man's salvation and the work of man in the world by which he demonstrates his sonship, the Protestant understanding of justification by faith frees man for the fullest utilization of his reason and makes him receptive to truth in whatever form it appears. Such faith prompts what Gogarten calls "questioning ignorance," that combination of certainty and openness, reverence and curiosity, which recognizes the importance but also the limitations of all human knowledge. Aware of his inability to create or control ultimate truth and goodness, man pursues the life of the mind with "a humility appropriate to this self-understanding."[5] He knows that human knowledge is always but an intimation of ultimate reality, "including its own uncertainty as an integral part of it."[6]

The recognition that faith in God is not threatened by the advances in knowledge, which displace God as a stop-gap, should encourage one to applaud the empowering of human reason in the assurance that Christians have no need to fear the emergence of any new truth, but can welcome it as evidence of man's increasing capacity to live in the world without dependence upon religious explanations.

On this basis, the church should welcome the proliferation of knowledge in which universities have played such a crucial role, the burgeoning of new fields of study, and the breadth of inquiry now possible because of extensive specialization in learning and research. Christians should affirm that mood in modern secular science which makes it possible to characterize this most potent determinant of contemporary life as possessed of a "new intellectual freedom and openness, sharpened sensitivities and creativity in the humanistic sense."[7] Instead of viewing science as a threat to faith, a monistic world-view which claims to interpret the only reality there is, the church must realize that modern science is a vastly different enterprise than its adversary during the "war between science and religion" in the late eighteenth century and the nineteenth century. In its insistence that increasing the known does not diminish the unknown, that its questions cannot be adequately answered by appealing to a simple and closed world, and that however much truth it does yield, the mystery remains inexhaustible, modern science represents a form of "questioning ignorance" which does not presume to dissolve all mystery, overlook its limitations, or absolutize its relative answers. And as the product of science, technology should also be recognized by the church as a manifestation of man's lordship over the world and viewed with a spirit of thankfulness, rather than parochial fear.

Expansion of the frontiers of human knowledge, diversification of disciplines, extension of fields of research, openness in modern science, and creativity in technology—all should be welcomed in higher education and seen as part of man's response to God's command to assume dominion over the world. Knowing that it is not by these means that salvation is secured, Christians are free to accept and use all of the fruits of human knowledge.

But the concomitant responsibility of the church to help protect the secularity of the university demands a recognition of and judgment upon the various forms of ideological reductionism prevalent there. For if man's freedom is genuine, his anxiety is inevitable, and when he is anxious the same powers which he uses for seeking truth are often perverted to self-justification, which substitutes dogmatism for openness of mind and the idolatry of the closed system for honest inquiry. Such reductionism occurs when it is claimed that there is actually only one proper method of finding the truth, or when disciplines construct premature syntheses and claim for their part the comprehensiveness of the whole.

In the past this totalitarian claim was often made by the natural or exact sciences, with their so-called "scientific worldview" and easy dismissal of the findings of other disciplines as "unscientific." The resulting scientism was justly deplored because of the final validity it claimed for its findings and its correlative claim that science provides everything that deserves to be termed "knowledge." Such a positivistic posture is more often found today among those social scientists who in their zeal to gain acceptance for their emerging disciplines explicitly or implicitly limit reality to that which can be measured or verified by their particular surveys or clinical methods. The church must protest against any such "nothing but" approach to truth, any effort to foreclose or limit knowledge by producing total explanations rather than illumination, and must insist upon the partiality of all human knowledge and the idolatry of any claim to provide truth in unconditioned or final form.

For this reason the church has a stake in the promotion of the liberal arts—not only because they aim at sensitizing persons to all that is human, helping them come to terms with and accept responsibility for themselves and their world, but also because such studies help to free persons from bondage to quantitative, measurable time, space, and matter. Such studies also tend to check epistemological monism by demonstrating that no single discipline can achieve the liberation of the mind. Humanistic studies help to balance the "technical reason" which permeates the current campus scene, i.e., the domination of means over ends and techniques over values. The pragmatism which characterizes the secular style of life can be prevented from degenerating into pure operationalism only when persons are not allowed to forget that there are other ways of establishing truth than utility, other dimensions of life than the useful. At a time when rapid technical innovation creates obsolescence for professional and specialized training, there is an even greater need to develop the attitude toward inquiry which the liberal arts make possible, an attitude which does not become obsolete. Thus a liberal education, which balances the arts and the sciences, can provide an occasion for students to understand the various approaches—humanistic, scientific, philosophical, mathematical, and theological—which men through the ages have taken in seeking knowledge. The liberal arts core curriculum should therefore be protected against any usurpation by specialized or professional education.

In like vein, the church should protest against the expulsion of wonder and awe from the life of the mind. Wherever the disenchantment and intellectualization which are characteristic of the process of secularization have led to the belief that all truth can be conceptualized, all things can be mastered by calculàtion, and the mysterious is to be expunged, Christians must label this a misunderstanding of the world's desacralization. The wonder, or "second naïvete" (Paul Ricoeur), which characterizes scientific research today is not the awe of ignorance but the post-Enlightenment wonder of those who know enough no longer to dare to regard all mysteries as problems which can be readily solved by proper techniques or reduced to manageable propositions.

At its best, liberal learning preserves the balance between the unknown viewed as a problem to be solved and as a mystery to be celebrated. It does this by reminding the sciences of their acknowledged limitations and by including those disciplines which respect and seek to celebrate, rather than deplore and seek to eliminate, the dimension of mystery from human life. As one spokesman for the humanities puts this,

> The view of things implicit in the work of the artist, as of the theologian, includes . . . the knowledge that it is a human approximation, a human penetration of order which lies beyond the human. The sense of mystery, almost of miracle involved in the proper study of the humanities results from a recognition of the way in which the known exists within the unknown, suggesting how one may regard that unknown but never usurping the place of deity by pretending to be the sum of things.[8]

So in addition to the mood of disciplined disengagement which is appropriate for conceptual analysis and problem-solving in the university, the church must encourage the cultivation of another mood appropriate for acknowledging the mysterious, nonrational dimension of reality. Without seeking to capture, dissolve, or capitulate to the nonrational, and yet never exhaustively understanding it, such a mood of "grateful wonder" acknowledges the depth and celebrates the power of the nonrational, resisting the ever present temptation to ignore it or to deplete its power and majesty with rational, causal explanations.

The church's concern to preserve the secular university's openness to all humanizing learning should also lead to criticism of the obscurantism which excludes the teaching of religion from its curriculum. An institution can be secular without succumbing to the kind of secularism which denies the significance of any dimension of human experience and regards the study of religion as superstitious and inappropriate in a liberal education. The reasons for this suspicion are valid enough. The theological imperialism and ecclesiastical hegemony which often characterized the teaching of religion in the past and prompted educators to regard it as a foreign agent bent on using or dominating the university are easily documented. The indoctrination, inspiration, and moralization which found their way into religion courses are well known. And the feeling persists that religion is not a genuine academic discipline because on epistemological grounds its basis in revelation and faith make "its claims and discourse by definition incompatible with the canons of inquiry accepted by the secular university."[9] The churches' isolation of theological education from the universities in denominational seminaries, the failure to distinguish between piety and scholarship, and the tendency to make theology an all-pervasive system which orders all other disciplines— these made the churches largely responsible for the expulsion of religion from the curriculum of the secular universities and represent a religious perversion of the process of secularization.

But this expulsion need not be final, and the very openness and integrity which secularity requires is being cited today as the basis for including the study of religion in general education and encouraging scholarly research in the field of religion. For when secular institutions fail to include the study of religion for fear of negative reactions from political or religious groups, they are evading their responsibility and compromising their autonomy. It has been repeatedly asserted in the last decade that on educational and academic grounds any university which claims concern for the totality of human experience should provide ample opportunity for the study of religion. It is on these grounds that the churches must work for the inclusion of the study of religion in higher education in order to help universities express their openness to all aspects of human reality and experience.

But in doing this, the church must also be clear as to the

basis on which religion is taught in the secular universities. It is easy enough to get general agreement that religion is a fundamental part of human experience and a formative influence in Western culture which should not be excluded from consideration in the community of learning. The question is, however, not *whether* religion should be studied, but *how* it can be included in the university in a way appropriate to its life.

In order to avert some of the suspicion that forced religion from the curriculum in the last century, it helps to make and maintain the distinction between the *teaching* of religion and the *practice* of religion, between the historical and critical approach in courses of study and the personal, existential approach in worship and witness. Of course instruction in religion will affect the personal convictions of students, but in the same way that an engaging course in English literature or contemporary philosophy might—by increasing their knowledge and by sharpening their critical faculties, not by making them any more religious, moral, or orthodox.

The study of religion uses the same methods of investigation as other disciplines—literary, historical, linguistic, and philosophical analysis. It differs primarily in content, in the nature of the material it studies, namely, that dimension of human experience traditionally designated "religion" and that body of literature which includes the beliefs, practices, and histories of the world's religions. Although it interacts with all other areas of human experience and employs methods common to the humanistic enterprise, as a field of scholarly study religion should be treated in a separate department if it is to gain recognition within the academic community.[10] Here it seeks no deferential treatment but simply the right to share with other disciplines in the preservation and extension of human knowledge.

The church must make plain, however, that it seeks a place for religion in the curriculum not as its "unifying principle," or as a means of improving campus morals or protecting students' faith, or as a bulwark against communism or any other ideology. It is motivated, rather, by its conviction that the absence of biblical understanding deprives the liberal arts of one important dimension which has contributed to the freeing of persons for a more truly human existence. The church's claim upon individual loyalties, its bid for existential commitment, and its proclamation of the saving work of God in Jesus Christ, in short its explicit call to faith—these it makes not in the classroom of the secular university, but in the context of its own worship and witness. This does not mean that the professor who is a churchman gives no evidence of his personal faith in the classroom. It is, rather, an effort to maintain a distinction between the proclamation of the gospel which is the basis for faith and the proper concern of the church, and the human knowledge which is the subject matter of religion and an appropriate concern of the university.

If commitment to the teaching and study of religion is to be distinguished from personal faith and commitment to the church, and the teaching of religion treated like any other discipline within the university, then the church has little cause to insist that religion be taught only by representatives of the Protestant, Roman Catholic, or Jewish traditions. A competent Jewish scholar may be the best teacher of contemporary Jewish thought, but because he is a competent scholar, not simply because he is Jewish. His Jewishness does not preclude his scholarly treatment of the church fathers, per se.

Even as the church insists upon the autonomy and integrity of the teaching of religion, it makes plain through its own worship and witness that the study of religion as an intellectual discipline does not exhaust it. The rational analysis of religion must never be allowed to become a substitute for the human experience of faith. So the church must maintain a ministry of its own within the university in which its members, lay and ordained, are reminded and remind others of that personal relationship to God which has been made possible in Jesus Christ and the ultimate meaning this provides. It does this best in the secular context not by reliance upon cultic proclamation in traditional religious language, but by engaging persons in theological reflection, summoning them to search for proximate meaning in the events and studies in which they are engaged.

Just as the church is concerned for the teaching of religion as a valid field of study and research within the university, it should also work for the inclusion of theology as one part within the broader field of religion in order that it be comprehensive.[11] Although the English and German universities make no distinction between the teaching of religion and theology, it is helpful to conceive of theological study somewhat more narrowly as systematic thinking on the basis of particular revelatory experiences. Theology, in turn, has been further divided into historical, or descriptive, theology and dogmatic, or constructive, theology. Although it is much easier to include the former in a department of religion in a "survey of religious thought" or "history of doctrine" course, the possibility of teaching systematic theology in secular institutions is now being explored on the basis that an ecumenical theological consensus is emerging which regards theology as the work of ordinary human reason which should not be disassociated from the university.[12]

Yet if the teaching of theology is to include the advocacy of a particular position, the church must reiterate that its aim is not the conversion of students or the reestablishment of theological sovereignty, but the opportunity to compete in the open market of conflicting ideas and to make whatever contribution theological reflection can to the university's exploration of all dimensions of truth. Thus theology can claim no privileged position in the secular university but only the standing earned by the efficiency, rigor, and relevancy of its academic practitioners. In addition, the church knows that theology stands to gain from its participation in the university milieu.

> . . . in our culture the university is the place where the various sciences exist in a common environment, with the possibility of many kinds of contact among those engaged in different lines of inquiry. . . . When [theology] is excluded the other sciences try to play its part as well as their own—with results that vary from the clumsy to the ludicrous. Where good theology is excluded, bad theology flourishes. Men will raise theological issues; theology might as well be there to tackle them. . . . [Theology] needs the university so that it will ask the right questions, the questions that keep it at the growing points of human knowledge and within the consciousness of contemporary man.[13]

If the church is to engage persons in the academic community in serious theological reflection on the meaning of their history, it must be willing to develop an understanding of theology which does not force the present into a framework from the past or divorce it from the secular world, but enables persons to discern their true humanness through engagement in the world of the present, in this case the world of ideas.

The church needs the university to give present relevance to its theology, and the university needs the church to remind it of the sources of its present secularity and to preserve that secularity from being destroyed by any external authority or internal ideology which would prevent it from remaining open to all forms of truth or dimensions of human experience.

Respect for the Relative Autonomies of University Disciplines

One of the contributions of the Christian faith to the process of secularization is the distinction it makes between faith as the result of God's actions in man's behalf and reason as man's work in behalf of the world. This distinction, which can be made on the basis of the Protestant understanding of justification by faith, emphasizes that freedom for God frees reason for its proper work of "discerning earthly-worldly meaning" and exposes its pretensions when it makes claims of ultimacy and seeks to usurp the place or function of faith. Hence faith "delivers" the world as God's creation over to man's reason and guarantees the autonomy of reason.[14]

If reason is regarded as "the organ of knowledge of the natural,"[15] as Bonhoeffer claimed, it is the responsibility of Christians to evidence "intellectual honesty," such "clean and honest use of reason" that it does not impose alien expectations upon penultimate structures, but sets them free for genuine worldliness and guards them against either religious answer-giving or ecclesiastical or political domination.

This can be done because of the difference between the ultimate significance of salvation which has its basis in faith and the earthly-worldly significance of human rationality.

. . . if we are not redeemed by a life of good works, no more are we redeemed by mental good works, by education, by brilliant thinking, or by having the correct thoughts and doctrines about God. The life of the mind is not the means by which we render ourselves acceptable before him . . . When one realizes that he is set right with God by grace alone, then he is liberated from the absurd necessity of trying to earn God's favor by what he does . . .[16]

As the means by which man fulfills his responsible sonship and evidences "true worldliness" human reason is assured full freedom in its conservation and extension of knowledge. Because reason is of a different order from faith, operating in a different area with a different function, human knowledge poses no threat to faith. Both liberate man, but the freedom of the Christian man is from guilt, anxiety, and any need to save himself, whereas the freedom of the liberally educated man is from ignorance, prejudice, and the limitations of his particular age and circumstances. Only when either faith or reason begins to make totalitarian claims—when faith tries to settle scientific or logical problems, or facts and logic are ascribed justifying power and claim to provide ultimate wholeness and meaning —does conflict arise.

In this context, the work of the university as the institution most responsible for the refinement and proliferation of human knowledge takes on tremendous importance as one area where man accepts his human responsibility to understand the world and to exercise his autonomous reason. So the church should applaud the freedom of investigation and research which higher education provides, the relative autonomy of its various disciplines, and the concern to keep every part of the academic community free from subjection to external, alien authority. As the domain of reason, not revelation, learning should be free from all theological domination. Affirming the ultimate coherence of all truth, the church thus seeks to preserve the freedom of inquiry, the immunity from alien domination, and the power of self-determination which autonomous reason requires.[17] It does this by maintaining the radical disjunction between God's action and those activities over which men have control, and by defending the arts and sciences against ecclesiastical or political supervision, or any other effort to impose a regulating principle.

The church therefore should applaud the relative autonomy

of the various disciplines within the university because of its respect for the integrity of the different orders of truth and its belief that the best research is possible only where there is no restricting fear or prejudice but freedom to pursue truth without limitations. This also suggests that the church should stop lamenting the multilingualness of the academic community and accept the varied rules which operate in the diverse "language games" of its disciplines. It also suggests that the church dare not be so presumptuous as to demand that all discussion of significant questions among faculty and students be in its religious categories or theological dialect, but recognize that questions of consequence are being considered daily in nonreligious terms. As one writer observes, "Until now, the temptation of the clergy has been to teach the laity to listen to them or talk the way they talk within the church. Now it is their job to help the laity learn to talk theologically, using the language of the world itself."[18]

But because knowledge is accumulated by persons whose vision is limited and whose exercise of reason is always conditioned by circumstance and bias, the church must also insist upon recognition of the inherent limitations of all human learning and renounce all pretense to ultimacy or absoluteness. Such a perspectival view of truth, which insists that no human assertions can be formulated absolutely, need not lead to skepticism and the belief that all assertions are arbitrary, or to subjectivism and the belief that all men are free to determine their own truth.[19] For to affirm that truth is known relatively is not to say that all truth is relative, but rather to acknowledge that is it always encountered in the concrete, conditioned context of human existence and articulated in the categories of a particular period. For instead of concluding from the incompleteness and relativity of all human knowing that the learning process is hopeless, the constructive or "theocentric relativism of biblical faith . . . preserves what is significant and vital in the relativistic emphasis, without permitting it to lapse into self-destroying absolutism,"[20] e.g., nihilism. The church underscores the interdependence and complementary nature of the several intellectual methods and disciplines within the university as it affirms their independence and autonomy.

And the church should applaud the sense of purpose which provides a unity to the university's life, even as it recognizes the apparent fragmentation of truth reflected in its compartmentalized and specialized curriculum. If the process of secularization contributed to the breakdown and repudiation of the metaphysical categories which provide a framework for interpreting all truth and thus encouraged the diversification of human knowledge, then a secular university can scarcely be expected to evidence a unified understanding of truth. But instead of bemoaning the brokenness of truth in the university, i.e., the diverse methods of verification, the technical languages, and the separate disciplines there, the church should affirm the dynamic differentiation in higher education.

Although the church affirms that truth is one and that in Jesus Christ all things hold together, it knows this in faith, as an eschatological hope, not an empirical reality to be proved in the academic community. It knows that human knowledge is never simple, univocal, and closed, but complex, ambiguous, and open, containing always a multiplicity of levels and spheres of truth, each with its own laws and requirements which must be acknowledged and respected. In the light of human creatureliness and finitude on the one hand and the vast diversity of human knowledge on the other hand, it is well to recall Roger Mehl's statement:

> The work of Christ has a hidden effect which will not appear until the end of time. The unity of truth is from our point of view a broken unity. We cannot coordinate all truth from our perspective. Knowledge in history must therefore be secular. The medieval dream of a total harmony of truth hierarchically ordered to one another is destroyed not only by the secularizing process, but by the nature of God's action in Christ itself.[21]

At present, the sense of the unity of truth and the assurance of its ultimate wholeness are part of the vision of faith, not any overarching scheme which can be imposed upon or developed out of the fragmented truths of the university.

> Our problem is not our inability to put the world together. It is that we want so desperately to put it together. The world coheres

in Christ. That is faith. It is religious arrogance or arrogance in any form to believe that one can put all things together. . . . We must abandon the notion that we do not know when we cannot put things together. . . . It is time to quit berating the fragmentation of knowledge. It is time rather to call upon men in their specialties to have a humane vision of life in its wholeness. Indeed the achievement of depth in each discipline, with openness to what is discovered and discerned in other areas, is the exciting possibility in the modern university.[22]

But along with its affirmation of the responsible use of reason in the academic community, its diversified and specialized truth-seeking, the integrity of its several disciplines, and the legitimate pluralism which this produces, the church has the correlative responsibility to protest against any efforts to pervert this autonomy.

Secular deterioration of the relative autonomy within the university's disciplines occurs whenever their relativity is denied or their autonomy is absolutized. The church's proper criticism begins thus with the university's failure to live up to its own secular claims, its inability to explore the full range of human inquiry because of the absolute claims of one or more of its disciplines. The "liberal rationalism" which Arnold Nash found permeating the American universities in the 1940's is a case in point.[23] The invasion of other disciplines by the positivistic method of the sciences is another illustration. Within a single discipline, the widespread insistence that linguistic analysis is the only appropriate way to "do philosophy" today is symptomatic of this same tendency to absolutize a method which has relative worth.

A second form in which the relativity of the disciplines is denied is the claim that they provide ultimate meaning and wholeness. While affirming the responsible exercise of reason and the pursuit of rational truth in the university, the church must question the soteriological claims of reason, or any "belief that intellectual knowledge brings benefits to human existence which are fundamentally redemptive."[24] Insisting upon the maintenance of the distinction between the salvation offered by God in faith and the responsible use of human reason, the church must question the claim of any discipline to reconcile man with the world or to provide him with ultimate truth. Knowledge need not be saving in order to be valuable. The academic disciplines provide contexts for taking seriously the penultimate structures of human life; they cannot and should not pretend to silence the "questioning ignorance" which is part of humanness or to provide the ultimate meaning which is integral to salvation.

The relativity of the disciplines is also denied by the refusal to recognize their operative presuppositions. Although the defensive claims to objectivity of the nineteenth and early twentieth centuries are seldom heard today, and there are few disciplines in which it is claimed that decisions are made or research conducted disinterestedly, there is still a certain reticence to acknowledge basic assumptions. The proper objectivity which should be defended seeks to penetrate to the level of "absolute presuppositions," there to compare and examine whether they make sense of human experience. But the false objectivity which should be exposed is the denial that commitment and accepted premises are integral to the learning process. Thus the responsibility of Christians within the university is to expose the various presuppositions, examining their status in order to understand the ultimate commitments which undergird the various disciplines.

The relativity of reason also is denied when it assumes responsibility for the wholeness of the world, a wholeness which is known only to God's creatorhood and saving action in Jesus Christ. At a time when so many persons are decrying the fragmentation in the modern university, it is not surprising that there are many efforts to provide some organizing principle. It should be the role of the church to expose the ideological presumption of any effort to impose an intellectual synthesis upon the university, for this not only violates the relative autonomy of the various disciplines, but ignores the finite limits of human knowledge and the piecemeal and fragmentary nature of life as we experience it.

But the church should be equally chary of all tendencies to reduce the Christian faith to a unifying world-view or total explanation into which the various bits of learning can be fitted. Although confidence in the wholeness of truth is part of the "fiduciary context" of Christian reflection, any effort to turn the Christian faith into an intellectual system alongside others is a form of theological imperialism which misunderstands the nature of faith and does violence to the relative autonomy of the reason. Man in a secular age should resist all attempts, Christian or otherwise, to formulate a totalistic explanation as premature efforts to impose unity which limit the autonomy of reason, on the one hand, and indicate lack of faith in God's power to make all things whole, on the other. It is the scholar's capacity to live with piecemeal, pragmatic, and limited truths without elevating any one of them to ultimacy which is in some sense the mark of his faith and acceptance of his finitude.

The secular university, with its structures for the exchange of knowledge, interdepartmental studies, and growing interdependence, finds its unity, therefore, not in ideological or theological categories, but in functional collaboration. The church should recognize that truth is unified by bringing it to bear on specific problems, as experts from various fields pool their specialized knowledge and pull the various strands of their experience together into a cord that will serve particular human needs.

But if it is not the function of the university or the church to reduce modern pluralism to unity by providing some unifying world-view, it *is* the responsibility of the university to make this pluralism intelligible and the task of the church to support it in this effort. The secularity of the university rests, therefore, not in some kind of demonstrable unification—ideological, political, or theological—but in the maintenance of a context in which the unique and necessary character of each discipline is recognized and respected and the disciplines work together in a complementary way—an atmosphere marked not by pride or imperialism, but by humility which is creative of genuine learning.

Concern for Faculty and Student Freedom and Responsibility

A third area in which the church should seek to protect the secularity of higher education is in the exercise of freedom and responsibility within the academic community. If certain insights of the Christian faith contributed to the demand for greater freedom and fuller responsibility in American colleges, as was argued above, then Christians have the responsibility of supporting subsequent efforts to protect these rights and increase this responsibility and to protest any abridgments or perversion of them.

The transformed self-understanding which arose out of the biblical understanding of the historicity of human existence, filial freedom, and human responsibility suggests not simply an explanation for what has happened in Western thought but also a continuing task for the church. A man "come of age" rejects slavish dependence upon or submission to oppressive regulations which deprive him of his self-constituting decision-making, and accepts responsibility for his own life and conduct. A person must be free from bondage to imposed regimentation before he can be truly responsible for his own existence.

Thus the church should applaud and encourage the development of faculty and student participation in certain academic decisions, especially acceptance of the concept of academic freedom which has given to faculty a measure of security and status and to students a sense of participation in higher education. Because academic freedom is a necessary condition for the free pursuit of knowledge, Christians should support the efforts of these groups to secure and protect the freedom of faculty to pursue research and share findings without interference so long as they evidence personal integrity and professional competence.

The church should oppose any prescribed tests for teachers, involving either their personal faith or political loyalties, for such tests put a premium on hypocrisy and seldom test the right things. The church should also work for participation of faculty in determination of university policy, convinced that professors' diverse disciplines and experience will contribute much to the shaping of higher education.

Because education is not simply indoctrination but a means of equipping persons for responsible exercise of their humanness, the church should also support the efforts of those groups seeking to promote responsible participation of students in the structures of higher education. In its concern to help students approximate mastery of themselves, the church should affirm efforts to do away with undue regimentation of student life, a vestige of colonial days which often restricts the learning process and treats students as irksome children who must be closely supervised. It should welcome the movement from punitive to more permissive policies, convinced that college-age adults are capable of accepting more responsibility for their actions than has been conceded by administrators in the past. And the church should support all efforts to develop responsible student participation in the formulation of policy through inclusion on faculty and administrative committees, in self-government and student judiciaries, and in those activities which sensitize them to social responsibility.

But at the same time, recognizing the many ways freedom gets forfeited, the church must emphasize that freedom from oppressive authority or paternalistic restraint does not mean freedom from accountability or freedom to do as one pleases. Freedom from elaborate codes of personal conduct means heightened responsibility for one's actions, increased accountability regarding the use of freedom. Hence the current student demands for freedom from excessive regulations can best be met by affording greater opportunity for participation in academic affairs and utilization of forms of negotiation and mediation consistent with the nature of the academic community. At no point should freedom from restraint be interpreted to mean freedom to not participate in the community of scholars.

The church must also emphasize the derivedness of freedom within the university, that it is not a natural and inalienable right which can be absolutized, but something entrusted to persons and easily forfeited through misuse. Theologically understood, human freedom is always developed over against another, and when that opposition is ignored or dissolved, the freedom itself is lost. In this sense, even as it deplores authoritarianism, the church should discourage total abdication of parental or institutional authority since that threatens freedom by removing the demands which make it possible. If students' freedom is derived and limited, not inherent or absolute, they should be reminded that they do not have the right to make decisions on all questions, regardless of competence, experience, and knowledge, in disregard of the rights and judgments of administration and faculty. Rather, theirs is a transactional, "fiduciary relationship" (E. C. Williamson) in which certain responsibilities are entrusted to them.

And because of the concern of the Christian faith for the whole person, the church should support all efforts to help faculty and students become self-directing, responsible persons outside as well as within the classroom. For this reason the church protests any depersonalization by the "multiversities" which decreases the sense of individual worth in faculty and students, heightens their feeling of being manipulated, and provokes demonstrations and protests in forms inconsistent with the life of the university as persons seek any means to overcome their sense of impotence and to recover some sense of power and meaning. Christians should support such efforts to rehumanize higher education as developing small residential colleges within larger universities, enlarging tutorial, advisory, and counseling programs, experimenting with "community government" approaches to campus life, and exploring the relation of the university to issues and movement beyond the campus. The church should also deplore the paternalism which deprives students and faculty of opportunities for self-determination and leaves them resentful and hostile toward the benevolent bureaucracy of the academic "Establishment."

In both faculty and student life, the church must encourage a balance between freedom and responsibility which prevents the perversion of the former by the constant reminder of the necessity of the latter, insisting that the university is failing in its basic mission to help persons learn to think and act in a truly human fashion if it does not provide a context in which freedom can be fully experienced and responsibility fully exercised.

Respect for Diversity in Institutional Forms and Goals

In spite of the spate of publications analyzing the academic community in recent years and proposing programs for clarifying its goals, there seems to be little agreement on just where American higher education is going or where it should go, even as it produces ever more alternative ways of getting somewhere. It is easy enough, therefore, in a theological discussion of higher education to put forward a clearly defined idea of the university and to suggest that the present chaos in our colleges can be attributed to failure to fulfill this normative image. Unfortunately, such a simplistic approach scarcely does justice to the historical development of higher education in this country, to the diversity which characterizes university life today, or to the insights suggested by this theological analysis of secularization. For the historical process which has been described here is one in which any definition of the essential nature of human institutions has been thrown into question by the emergence of diversity of thought and plurality of forms.

Thus instead of finding in the recent theological thought concerning secularization any clear idea of what a secular university —or any other secular institution—should be, we find only suggestions of what constitutes secularity, or "true worldliness," and hence deserves to be protected against perversion by secularism, or spurious worldliness. To be "emancipated for true worldliness" means for secular institutions to be freed from any alien rule or external authority and to be able to attain their own true character and be subject to their own innate law.

This demands a repudiation of the church's claim to externally imposed authority over secular institutions and implies that universities, though initially children of the churches, have now achieved a measure of autonomy with their maturity, making them capable of self-determination and freedom from denominational tutelage. It also suggests that the role of Christians within the university is to ally themselves with those forces seeking to preserve its secularity.

> . . . as the franchise is the sign of political adulthood, so the university's assertion of its freedom from theological governance was the sign that it too claims the rights that belong to maturity. And no warnings about the hazards of the adult life will induce the university-come-of-age to tie itself again to the apron strings of Mother Church. . . . it is as dangerous for the theologian to have power over intellectual life as for the church hierarchy to dominate the political order.[25]

This means, first of all, defending the autonomy of the university as an institution in society and recognizing that it can best be true to its own purposes by being independent of both church and state. If the work of Christ frees the orders of creation for their own allotted functions, and if the purpose of the universities is quite different from that of the church or the state, then there is no reason for the church or the state to dominate higher education.

The church best serves the university, in this sense, by seeking to protect it from all efforts—ecclesiastical, financial, or political—to usurp its freedom, shape its curriculum, or influence its teaching. It should oppose legislative "speaker ban" laws and congressional investigations with the same zeal with which it opposes sectarian heresy hunts and demands for the dismissal of controversial faculty members. Individual Christians best preserve the integrity of the university by working through the appropriate channels to assure the appointment of responsible and capable trustees for guiding institutions according to their own self-understanding.

A second way the secularity of higher education can be affirmed is in eschewing any single idea of the university. Although there is a qualitative standardization of the work done in the European universities, in the United States there are only regional accrediting organizations which define institutional accreditation in the broadest possible terms. Hence there is a tendency to designate a great variety of institutions "universities" and to reject any attempt to stipulate what constitutes a "true" university. The generic category "university" embraces such a variety of institutions and is subject to such constant change that to propose any single ideal concept suggesting uniformity or constancy would be illusory.

Instead of insisting upon some unchanging "idea" of the university or attempting to measure institutions by some essential "universityness," the church should recognize and affirm the increasing variety, diversity, and pluralism of higher education today. The enormous diversity of needs which characterize our differentiated society calls for many different kinds of education and institutions, large and small, public and private, general and specialized, not conformity to some one academic ideal. In spite of its historic identification with small liberal arts colleges, the church must cease its nostalgic longing for the academic simplicity of the colonial era and accept the validity of the educational task being carried out in large technological schools, state teachers' colleges, and metropolitan multiversities, recognizing that different types of schools have important contributions to make to higher education.

> Diversity in the university world provides us a basis for affirming the freedom and relative autonomy of these institutions. They need not all do the same things to be called universities; they must, instead, be held responsible for determining with clarity what they shall do and the procedures by which their ends shall be sought. Despite the clamouring for a single "idea of the university" and the desire for some uniform set of standards by which the quality of university education may be judged, the fact that universities are different, have different histories and functions with respect to the world around them, is an enriching of the whole of the university tradition and of modern life.[26]

Although there are certain standards to which a university may be held accountable, these should be goals it sets for itself on the basis of its history, sponsorship, size, endowment, and aims, not those imposed from without by external authorities. Hence any judgment which the church pronounces upon a university must be based upon its own stated aims, and not be derived from an 1850 English model proposed by John Henry Newman, or even a 1940 German model proposed by Karl Jaspers, or a 1960 American model projected by Clark Kerr.

The absence of a clear objective standard by which to measure a university's effectiveness suggests that the church's role as "friendly critic" within the academic community is best fulfilled by university personnel who are identified with it and know its aims and claims, rather than by itinerant preachers or visiting speakers. Judgment is in order whenever an institution becomes so vulnerable either to pressures from within (particular personalities or disciplines which exert an imperialism disproportionate to their human importance) or to pressures from without (political authorities, religious movements, student protest groups, business interests, or financial benefactors) that its common life is misshaped and the autonomy and integrity which constitute its secularity are threatened. The "positive neutrality" which is the mark of a secular university should be affirmed as providing a preferred status to no single position, religious or nonreligious, rational or revealed, private or institutional, prevalent or esoteric; it should be criticized when it degenerates into a "malevolent neutrality" which gives the impression that any position is insignificant or untrue by omitting it from consideration.

The church is also rightly critical of any effort to impose external criteria upon the university, that is, any insistence that its faculty and students be loyal, patriotic, religious, or committed according to some predetermined standard. This has been done often enough in the recent history of American higher education by sectarian and political zealots to make this a genuine and continuing concern of educators today. But this has also been done by well-intentioned educators and theologians who developed ontological notions of what constitutes *the* university and then sought to recall particular institutions to that substantialistic norm. On the basis of such a definition, Abraham Flexner could contend in 1930 that "neither Columbia, nor Harvard, nor Johns Hopkins, nor Chicago, nor Wisconsin is really a university, for none of them possesses unity of purpose or homogeneity of constitution."[27] Other writers have called the university to its "true and proper function" using some other norm like Oxford, Harvard, or the University of Paris, instead of the German model which Flexner envisaged. But if the church honestly believes that the secular university has a genuine worldliness of its own, then it will resist all efforts to impose a single "idea of the university" on radically diverse institutions. Rather, Christians will respect each institution's understanding of its nature and role, seek to discern the dynamics of its life, and participate in its purposes.

> Instead of trying to recapture a lost unity of faith and knowledge, or to entice the university back into medieval patterns, or to devise new and ingenious schemes for more status for religion on campus, or to

promote the readoption of old postulates, the first questions must be, "What has God been doing with his house of intellect while we were looking backward, or seeking our institutional advantage?"[28]

This means that the church should also question the kind of other-directedness which characterizes intellectual and educational leaders today and keeps them frantically trying to copy the institutions just above them on the prestige scale in this day of mass education. At a time when higher education has successfully permeated our national culture and our universities are overflowing with students, Christians have the responsibility of discerning for themselves the unique task of their particular university and helping it fulfill its professed purposes, rather than frantically trying to live up to a normative image imposed from outside. If the secular universities are to fulfill their unique responsibility and not succumb to the educational gimmickry and crude utilitarianism which threaten them, they must be protected against all efforts to reduce them to corporate, suburban, or military establishments and all attempts to view them as "knowledge factories" for producing "professional licences and apprentices for technological corporations, and to do extra-mural contracted research."[29] The church must therefore respect the diversity of institutional forms and goals in higher education, and through its members within the universities and its ministry to universities, help them be faithful to their unique calling within the variety which characterizes American higher education today.

Conclusion

The term "secularization" was first used to refer to the transfer of physical properties from ecclesiastical control to worldly principalities. Its subsequent use became tied to a heteronomous view of authority and a medieval view of reality which was based upon a static ontology, a view of God as an explanation, and an understanding of history as the realization of a divine, eternal plan within the world.

Today these concepts of medieval theology have become unserviceable for modern man because the world is viewed quite differently, as something for which man is to accept responsibility through modern science and technology. Faith is understood in a fundamentally different way as what occurs between God and man; reason has been granted a relative autonomy; and history is understood as that for which man bears responsibility, in which he determines who he is.

Therefore, because the constituent notions contained within the term "secularization"—world, reality, history, and authority—are understood in a different way today from the time in which the word was first used and its subsequent use in Protestant scholasticism, the function and hence the meaning of the term itself has changed. That this change has not been generally recognized explains the ambiguity which surrounds its use today.

In exploring the suspicion that recent efforts to formulate a "theology of the secular" might provide a suggestive way for reappraising the relation of religion to higher education and the place of the church in the universities, this study has sought to do justice to the theological insights of two contemporary German theologians, Friedrich Gogarten and Dietrich Bonhoeffer, while at the same time not violating the unique history and integrity of American higher education. Thus, rather than forcing the facts or problems to fit an imported theological scheme, the intention has been to see how a theological analysis of recent intellectual history illumines the problems which have arisen during the development of colleges and universities in the United States and suggests a posture for Christian faithfulness within secular higher education today. The problems raised have far outnumbered the solutions suggested, for such a study does not lend itself to solutions but to awareness and insight.

If secularization is in fact a continuing process rooted in faith and in some sense the responsibility of men of faith, then the gravest error would be to conclude that this process can be stopped at any point, finalized in any way, or that there is any absoluteness in the secularized forms it produces. The secular university which has emerged from the secularization of American higher education cannot itself be considered normative, but must be seen rather as a historically conditioned form which seeks to provide persons a context of freedom and responsibility commensurate with the demands of their maturity.

The future of the secular university will be determined in large part by how effective it is in maintaining an openness to all truth, protecting the relative autonomy of its disciplines, encouraging responsible participation by its faculty and students, and recognizing a diversity of institutional forms and goals. This, in turn, will be determined in large part by how effective persons within these institutions are in protecting their "genuine worldliness" and developing forms by which to fulfill academic responsibility. It is the conclusion of this study that Christians have an important stake in this process and are called by the very nature of their faith to participate in and help protect the openness and integrity of secular higher education as they discover a stance in relation to the university which is grounded in both the Christian faith and the secular world.

Notes

Chapter 1

1. "Secular," *Catholic Encyclopedia* (New York: Robert Appleton Co., 1912), Vol. XIII, pp. 677-678.

2. George Jacob Holyoake, *English Secularism: A Confession of Belief* (Chicago: Open Court Publishing Co., 1896), pp. 34 f.

3. Charles West, "Toward an Understanding of Secularism," *Religion and Society*, Vol. IX, No. 1 (March 1962), pp. 47-49.

4. J. V. Langmead Casserley, *The Bent World* (New York: Oxford University Press, 1955), p. 243.

5. Stanley Romaine Hopper, *The Crisis of Faith* (Nashville: Abingdon-Cokesbury Press, 1944), p. 33.

6. "The best examples of this kind of secularization are the Pantjasila of Indonesia and the secular socialist state of India. . . . In both India and Indonesia there is an attempt to affirm traditional culture, while insisting that in the interests of nation-building there must be acceptance of common social values. A secular social philosophy has resulted based on the idea that society and religion are, at least at certain points, distinct and separable, and should be so," Paul Abrecht has written in *The Churches and Rapid Social Change* (Garden City, N.Y.: Doubleday & Co., 1961), p. 202.

7. From a declaration of the cardinals and archbishops of France in 1945, reproduced in *Documentation Catholique* (January 1946) and quoted in André Latreille, "The Catholic Church and the Secular State," *Cross Currents*, Vol. XIII, No. 2 (Spring 1963), pp. 238, 239.

8. E.g., Peter L. Berger, *The Noise of Solemn Assemblies* (Garden City, N.Y.: Doubleday & Co., 1961), especially Ch. V, "Postscript on Commitment"; and Harvey Cox, *The Secular City* (New York: The Macmillan Co., 1965), especially ch. 10 on "The Church and the Secular University."

9. See Carl Michalson, *The Hinge of History* (New York: Charles Scribner's Sons, 1959), especially Part I; and Larry Shiner, *The Secularization of History* (Nashville: Abingdon Press, 1966).

Chapter 2

1. Larry Shiner's excellent introduction to the theology of Gogarten, titled *The Secularization of History*, analyzes his major themes and illustrates the pervasiveness and dominance of his concern for secularization.

2. Friedrich Gorgarten, *Verhängnis und Hoffnung der Neuzeit* (Stuttgart: Friedrich Vorwerk Verlag, 1953), 7, hereafter referred to as *Verhängnis*. Based on the English translation in manuscript form by Fred Paddock in consultation with Gogarten.

3. Gogarten, *Der Mensch zwischen Gott und Welt* (3rd ed.; Stuttgart: Friedrich Vorwerk Verlag, 1956), 139 (author's translation).

4. *Verhängnis,* 8.

5. Gogarten, *The Reality of Faith,* tr. Carl Michalson and others (Philadelphia: The Westminster Press, 1959), p. 40. This is the English translation of *Die Wirklichkeit des Glaubens: Zum Problem des Subjektivismus in der Theologie* (Stuttgart: Friedrich Vorwerk Verlag, 1957), cited hereafter as *Reality.*

6. *Der Mensch zwischen Gott und Welt,* 146–147.

7. *Reality,* pp. 168, 171, 172.

8. *Verhängnis,* 75.

9. *Ibid.,* 12.

10. Gerhard Ebeling, *The Nature of Faith,* tr. Ronald Gregor Smith (Philadelphia: Muhlenberg Press, 1961), p. 161.

11. *Reality,* pp. 60, 69.

12. *Der Mensch zwischen Gott und Welt,* 190-196.

13. *Reality,* p. 167.

14. *Ibid.,* p. 105.

15. Ebeling points out that this led to "the understandable yet quite devastating way in which the churches, both Protestant and Roman Catholic . . . in the name of Christian faith opposed insights which were undoubtedly true, and which in the end were triumphant in any case; suppressed the right of free inquiry; misled men's consciences; established the unavoidable stumbling-block of faith in quite the wrong place, and thus brought into confusion not only the understanding of faith but also the love of truth and truthfulness." *Op. cit.,* p. 80.

16. *Reality,* p. 104.

17. *Verhängnis,* 102.

18. Gogarten, *Demythologizing and History* (London: SCM Press, 1955), p. 21. English translation by Neville Horton Smith of *Entmythologisierung und Kirche* (Stuttgart: Friedrich Vorwerk Verlag, 1953).

19. *Ibid.,* p. 23.

20. *Der Mensch zwischen Gott und Welt,* 142.

21. *Reality,* p. 23.

22. *Verhängnis,* 142. Charles West translates this phrase "expectant relativity" in "Toward an Understanding of Secularism," *Religion and Society,* Vol. IX, No. 1 (March 1962), p. 60.

23. *Ibid.,* 143. Cf. Cox's explication of this distinction in *The Secular City,* pp. 20-21, 86, and Gayraud Wilmore's distinction between "spurious secularism" and "true secularity" in *The Secular Relevance of the Church* (Philadelphia: The Westminster Press, 1962), *passim.*

24. *Der Mensch zwischen Gott und Welt,* 151 ff., 154 ff.

25. *Verhängnis,* 143.

26. Martin Marty makes the same distinction between "secularization" which is "not necessarily integral or closed to faith" and "secularism" which is "self-contained, self-explanatory, self-enclosed," permitting "no witness to the activity of God in history, no possibility of 'belief *that*' he is or 'belief *in*' his actions or belief in the witnesses to him in the human sphere," in *Varieties of Unbelief* (New York: Holt, Rinehart and Winston, 1964), p. 145.

27. *Der Mensch zwischen Gott und Welt,* 147.

28. *Verhängnis,* 144.

29. Stephen Pepper, *World Hypotheses* (Berkeley: University of California Press, 1942), pp. 91, 96.

30. H. Richard Niebuhr, *The Responsible Self* (New York: Harper & Row, 1963), pp. 57-65.

31. Dietrich Bonhoeffer, *Prisoner for God* (New York: The Macmillan Co., 1953), p. 61. This is the English translation by Reginald H. Fuller of *Widerstand und Ergebung—Briefe und Aufzeichnungen aus der Haft* (Munich: Chr. Kaiser Verlag, 1955), which is also published as *Letters and Papers from Prison.* Copyright, 1953, by The Macmillan Company. Used by permission of The Macmillan Co. and SCM Press.

32. Bonhoeffer, *Ethics* (New York: The Macmillan Co.; London: SCM Press, 1955), pp. 32-33, 41. English translation by N. Horton Smith of *Ethik* (Munich: Chr. Kaiser Verlag, 1949). Copyright © 1955 by The Macmillan Company. Used by permission of The Macmillan Co. and SCM Press.

33. Bonhoeffer used this phrase in preference to "secularization," according to Hans Heinrich Brunner, in order to avoid the usual implication that this is a godless age in contrast to an earlier, entirely Christian one, assuming that "secularization" would be interpreted to mean "de-Christianization," instead of "de-religionization." "Am Ende des religiösen Zeitalters," *Reformatio,* IV, issue 8 (August 1955), 422.

34. Immanuel Kant, *What Is Enlightenment?,* tr. Lewis W. Beck (Chicago: University of Chicago Press, 1959), p. 86.

35. *Ethics,* p. 32.

36. *Prisoner for God,* p. 163.

37. *Ibid.,* p. 164. Jean Lacroix's penetrating discussion of modern atheism observes that one "can only deny a particular representation of God in the name of a more elevated representation." Lacroix applauds the kind of atheism which rejects all false gods—the gods of traditional spiritualism and idealism and other forms in which God has been compromised—and demands the continual purification of our representation of God. At this point he would probably label Bonhoeffer's effort a "methodological atheism," since it rejects "God as an explanation even while retaining him as meaning and presence." "The Meaning and Value of Atheism Today," *Cross Currents,* Vol. V, No. 3 (Summer 1955), pp. 205, 218.

38. *Prisoner for God,* pp. 145, 146.

39. "The First Table of the Ten Commandments," in John D. Godsey, *Preface to Bonhoeffer* (Philadelphia: Fortress Press, 1965), p. 60.

40. Clifford Green, "Bonhoeffer's Concept of Religion," *Union Seminary Quarterly Review,* Vol. XIX, No. 1 (November 1963), p. 21.

41. *Prisoner for God,* p. 126.

42. *Ibid.,* p. 179, incorporating Bethge's translation in preference to Fuller's rendering of this as "the nearest *thing* to hand." See *Chicago Theological Seminary Register,* Vol. LI, No. 2 (February 1961), p. 32.

43. *Ethics,* p. 62.

44. John A. T. Robinson, *Honest to God* (Philadelphia: The Westminster Press, 1963), pp. 84-85.

45. *Ethics,* p. 263.

46. *Prisoner for God,* p. 125.

47. Peter L. Berger, *The Precarious Vision* (Garden City, N.Y.: Doubleday & Co., 1961), p. 183.

48. *Prisoner for God*, p. 125.

49. *Ibid.*, p. 147.

50. *Ibid.*, pp. 142-143.

51. *Ibid.*, p. 126.

52. *Ibid.*, pp. 153, 154.

53. *Ibid.*, p. 122.

54. *Ibid.*, pp. 140-141.

55. Eberhard Bethge, "The Challenge of Dietrich Bonhoeffer's Life and Theology," *Chicago Theological Seminary Register*, Vol. LI, No. 2 (February 1961), pp. 34-35. Also available as Ch. II in *World Come of Age*, ed. Ronald Gregor Smith (Philadelphia: Fortress Press, 1967), pp. 81-82.

56. Will Herberg, *Protestant, Catholic, Jew* (Garden City, N.Y.: Doubleday & Co., 1955), especially Ch. V.

57. Paul Tillich, *Dynamics of Faith* (New York: Harper & Bros., 1957), especially Chs. I and IV.

58. See Walter Kaufmann, *Critique of Religion and Philosophy* (Garden City, N.Y.: Doubleday Anchor Book, 1961), pp. 100 ff.

59. John D. Godsey, *The Theology of Dietrich Bonhoeffer* (Philadelphia: The Westminster Press, 1960), p. 108.

60. *Dein Reich Komme* Furche-Bücherei, issue 146, 5 f. Quoted by Bethge, "The Editing and Publishing of the Bonhoeffer Papers," English translation in *The Andover Newton Bulletin*, Vol. LII, No. 2 (December 1959), p. 23. (Complete English translation available in *Preface to Bonhoeffer*, pp. 27-47.)

61. *Ethics*, p. 65.

62. *Prisoner for God*, p. 179.

63. *Ethics*, p. 262.

64. *Ibid.*, pp. 10, 20.

65. *Prisoner for God*, p. 166.

66. *Ethics*, p. 217.

67. Bonhoeffer, *Creation and Fall*, tr. John C. Fletcher (New York: The Macmillan Co., 1959), p. 38. English translation of *Schöpfung und Fall: Theologische Auslegung von Genesis 1—3* (Munich: Chr. Kaiser Verlag, 1933).

68. *Ethics*, p. 200.

69. *Ibid.*, pp. 293-294.

70. *Prisoner for God*, p. 169.

71. *Ethics*, p. 263.

72. *Ibid.*, p. 190.

73. *Ibid.*, p. 90.

74. *Ibid.*, p. 91, author's italics.

75. *Ibid.*, p. 100.

Chapter 3

1. Bonhoeffer, *Ethics*, p. 65.

2. Alexandre Koyré, *From the Closed World to the Infinite Universe* (Baltimore: Johns Hopkins Press, 1956), p. viii.

3. Ernst Cassirer, *The Philosophy of the Enlightenment* (Princeton: Princeton University Press, 1951), p. 65.

4. Basil Willey, *The Seventeenth Century Background* (Garden City, N.Y.: Doubleday Anchor Book, 1953), p. 16.

5. Abraham Wolf, *A History of Science, Technology, and Philosophy in the Sixteenth and Seventeenth Centuries* (New York: The Macmillan Co., 1935), p. 3.

6. Alfred N. Whitehead, *Science and the Modern World* (New York: The Macmillan Co., 1926), 1954 ed., p. 12.

7. Michael Foster, "The Christian Doctrine of Creation and the Rise of Modern Science," *Mind*, Vol. XLIII (October 1934), pp. 446-468; "Christian Theology and the Modern Science of Nature," Part I, *Mind*, Vol. XLIV (October 1935), pp. 439-466, and Part II, Vol. XLV (January 1936), pp. 1-27.

8. Robert K. Merton, "Puritanism, Pietism, and Science," *The Sociological Review*, Vol. XXXVIII, No. 1 (January 1936), pp. 29-30. Cf. John Dillenberger, *Protestant Thought and Natural Science* (Garden City, N.Y.: Doubleday & Co., 1960), pp. 128 ff.

9. Mary B. Hesse, *Science and the Human Imagination* (London: SCM Press, 1954), p. 162.

10. Gogarten, *Der Mensch zwischen Gott und Welt*, 150-151.

11. See Basil Willey, *The Eighteenth Century Background* (Boston: Beacon Press, 1940), especially Ch. I.

12. Will Herberg, "Faith and Secular Learning," in *Christian Faith and Social Action*, ed. John A. Hutchison (New York: Charles Scribner's Sons, 1953), p. 205. Throughout this article Herberg affirms the basic presuppositions of the scientific outlook while pointing out their propensity to perversion.

13. Michael Foster, *Mystery and Philosophy* (London: SCM Press, 1957), pp. 41-91. Cf. E. L. Mascall, *Words and Images* (London: Longmans, Green and Co., 1957), pp. 77 ff.

14. Myron B. Bloy, Jr., *The Crisis of Cultural Change* (New York: Seabury Press, 1965), pp. 100, 104, 105.

15. Myron B. Bloy, Jr., "The Gracefulness of Technology," *The Church Review*, Vol. XXII, Nos. 2-3 (April-May 1964), pp. 3-4.

16. Bloy, *The Crisis of Cultural Change*, p. 111.

17. Cornelis A. van Peursen, "Man and Reality—the History of Human Thought," *Student World*, Vol. LVI, No. 1 (1st Quarter 1963), pp. 13-21.

18. Cf. Richard Taylor, *Metaphysics* (Englewood Cliffs, N.J.: Prentice-Hall, 1963); D. F. Pears (ed.), *The Nature of Metaphysics* (New York: St. Martin's Press, 1957); and Gottfried Martin, *An Introduction to General Metaphysics* (London: Allen & Unwin, Ltd., 1961).

19. Frederick C. Copleston, "The Nature and Function of Metaphysics," *Philosophy*, Vol. XXVIII (January 1953), p. 5.

20. Frederick Ferré seeks to establish criteria for grading metaphysical systems in the final pages of *Language, Logic and God* (New York: Harper & Bros., 1961), pp. 162 ff.

21. J. V. Langmead Casserley's entire work, *The Christian in Philosophy* (London: Faber and Faber Ltd., 1949), is an effort to make a convincing case for "dramatic metaphysics," traced through Augustine, Anselm, and

Kierkegaard, over "serene metaphysics," stemming from Plato, and running through Aristotle, Plotinus, and Thomas Aquinas.

22. Cassirer, *op. cit.*, p. 80.

23. John Dillenberger, "On Broadening the New Hermeneutic," in *The New Hermeneutic* ("New Frontiers in Theology," Vol. II), eds. James M. Robinson and John B. Cobb, Jr. (New York: Harper & Row, 1964), p. 156.

24. Richard Hofstadter, *Academic Freedom in the Age of the College* (New York: Columbia University Press, 1955), pp. 17, 32.

25. Harry O. Morton, "The Mastery of Technological Civilization," *Student World*, Vol. LVI, No. 1 (1st Quarter 1963), p. 46.

26. Charles West, in Report on Consultation on "The Meaning of the Secular," Ecumenical Institute, Celigny, Switzerland, September 15-20, 1959 (Geneva: World Student Christian Federation). Mimeographed, p. 7.

27. Gogarten, *Verhängnis*, 7.

28. Sir Walter Moberly, *The Crisis in the University* (London: SCM Press, 1949), pp. 279-281. Cf. Martin Jarrett-Kerr's chronicling of the same process in ch. 2 of *The Secular Promise* (Philadelphia: Fortress Press, 1964), pp. 29-60.

29. West, in Report on Consultation, *op. cit.*, p. 8. Arnold Nash labels this "liberal rationalism" in his discussion of the unexamined presuppositions of American higher education in the 1940's, *The University and the Modern World* (New York: The Macmillan Co., 1943), *passim*.

30. Gerhard Ebeling, *Word and Faith* (London: SCM Press, 1963), p. 45.

31. Casserley, *The Christian in Philosophy*, p. 22.

32. Carl Michalson, *The Rationality of Faith* (New York: Charles Scribner's Sons, 1963), pp. 64-65.

33. Nicolas Berdyaev, *The Beginning and the End* (New York: Harper & Bros., 1957), pp. 114-115.

34. Will Herberg, "Biblical Faith as *Heilsgeschichte*," *The Christian Scholar*, Vol. XXXIX, No. 1 (March 1956), pp. 26-27.

35. *Prisoner for God*, p. 179.

36. E. Harris Harbison's description of growing historical consciousness in the Renaissance in *The Christian Scholar in the Age of the Reformation* (New York: Charles Scribner's Sons, 1956), p. 36.

37. Gogarten, *Reality*, p. 23.

38. Gogarten, *Demythologizing and History*, p. 20.

39. Emil Fackenheim, *Metaphysics and Historicity* (Milwaukee: Marquette University Press, 1961), p. 7.

40. Hans H. Walz, "Säkularisierung," *Weltkirchenlexikon* (Stuttgart: Kreuz-Verlag, 1960), 1289 f.

41. Ernst Troeltsch, *Protestantism and Progress* (Boston: Beacon Press, 1958), p. 18.

42. Martin Marty, *Second Chance for American Protestants* (New York: Harper & Row, 1963), p. 71.

43. Gibson Winter, *The New Creation as Metropolis* (New York: The Macmillan Co., 1963), p. 38.

44. *Reality*, p. 91.

45. *Ibid.*, pp. 87-88.

46. *Ethics*, p. 293.

47. Paul Tillich, *The Protestant Era* (Chicago: University of Chicago Press, 1948), pp. 213-214.

48. Christopher Dawson, *The Crisis of Western Education* (New York: Sheed and Ward, 1961), pp. 103, 161.

49. George H. Williams, *Wilderness and Paradise in Christian Thought* (New York: Harper & Bros., 1962), p. 166.

50. *Ibid.*, p. 171. The late Alexander Miller based his discussion of the proper relationship between church and university upon this distinction in *Faith and Learning* (New York: Association Press, 1960), pp. 66 ff.

51. Winter, *op. cit.*, pp. 43-44, 46-47, 48.

Chapter 4

1. Donald G. Tewksbury, *The Founding of American Colleges and Universities Before the Civil War* (New York: Teachers College, Columbia University, 1932), pp. 56-58.

2. E.g., Richard Butler, *God and the Secular Campus* (Garden City, N.Y.: Doubleday & Co., 1963).

3. Although the Civil War era and the founding of Johns Hopkins University in 1876 mark the transition from "the age of the college" to "the age of the university" in America, and the addition of graduate education is usually considered the factor primarily responsible for transforming liberal arts "colleges" into "universities," the terms are used here interchangeably in the generic sense of "institutions of higher education" without reference to any essentialistic notion of what constitutes a "true university" and distinguishes it from a "college."

4. See Martha Ornstein, *The Role of Scientific Societies in the Seventeenth Century* (Chicago: University of Chicago Press, 1938), for a discussion of the founding of such societies as the Academia Secretorum Naturae at Naples (1560), the Royal Society or "Invisible College" (1660), the Académie des Sciences (1666), and the Berlin Academy (1700), all protests in some sense against the refusal of universities to welcome scientific experimentation.

5. Nash, *The University and the Modern World*, p. 64.

6. Noah Edward Fehl, *The Idea of a University in East and West* (Hong Kong: Chung Chi College, 1962), p. 100. For John Henry Newman's reasons for excluding research from the academic community see *The Idea of a University* (New York: Holt, Rinehart & Winston, 1959), p. xi of the Preface.

7. R. Freeman Butts, *The College Charts Its Course* (New York: McGraw-Hill Book Co., 1939), p. 55.

8. Frederick Rudolph, *The American College and University* (New York: Alfred A. Knopf, 1962), p. 25.

9. Theodore Hornberger, *Scientific Thought in the American Colleges* (Austin: University of Texas Press, 1945), p. 40.

10. Louis F. Snow, *The College Curriculum in the United States* (New York: Columbia University Press, 1907), pp. 66 f.

11. Rudolph, *op. cit.*, p. 222.

12. Hofstadter, *Academic Freedom in the Age of the College*, p. 196.

13. Walter P. Metzger, *Academic Freedom in the Age of the University* (New York: Columbia University Press, 1955), p. 10.

14. Quoted in *ibid.*, p. 86.

15. Denis Baly, *Academic Illusion* (Greenwich, Conn.: Seabury Press, 1961), pp. 104-105.

16. Rudolph, *op. cit.*, p. 347.

17. Metzger, *op. cit.*, p. 72.

18. *Ibid.*, pp. 13-14.

19. Irving Babbitt, *Literature and the American College* (New York: Houghton Mifflin and Co., 1908), p. 136.

20. John H. Hallowell, "The Christian in the University," *motive* (March 1963), p. 40.

21. Butts, *op. cit.*, p. 25.

22. *Ibid.*, p. 29.

23. Quoted in E. Harris Harbison, "Liberal Education and Christian Education," in *The Christian Idea of Education*, ed. Edmund Fuller (New Haven: Yale University Press, 1957), p. 61.

24. *Ibid.*

25. Roland M. Frye, "Protestantism and Education: A Preliminary Study of the Early Centuries and Some Suggested Principles," study document for the National Council of Churches, New York. Mimeographed, pp. 11, 50.

26. *Ibid.*, pp. 30, 34, 35.

27. Samuel Eliot Morison, *The Founding of Harvard College* (Cambridge: Harvard University Press, 1935), p. 58.

28. Butts, *op. cit.*, p. 47.

29. Noting "the strength that it gave to the forces of reaction," Rudolph observes, "Behind it the American college curriculum remained almost immovable until after the Civil War." *Op. cit.*, pp. 132, 135.

30. Richard Hofstadter and Wilson Smith, eds., *American Higher Education: A Documentary History* (Chicago: University of Chicago Press, 1961), Vol. I, p. 278. The text of the report is to be found in "Original Papers in Relation to a Course of Liberal Education," *The American Journal of Science and Arts*, Vol. XV (January 1829), pp. 297-351, and is available in part in *American Higher Education*.

31. W. H. Cowley, *Introduction to American Higher Education* (Stanford: Stanford University, 1957), processed lecture notes, pp. 202-203.

32. Quoted in Rudolph, *op. cit.*, pp. 249, 252.

33. *Ibid.*, p. 294.

34. E. D. Phillips, "The Elective System in American Education," *Pedagogical Seminary*, Vol. VIII (June 1901), pp. 206-230.

35. Rudolph, *op. cit.*, p. 305.

36. Clark Kerr, *The Uses of the University* (Cambridge: Harvard University Press, 1963), pp. 14-15.

37. Babbitt, *op. cit.*, *passim.*

38. Abraham Flexner, *Universities: American, English, German* (New York: Oxford University Press, 1930), p. 179.

39. Rudolph, *op. cit.*, p. 480. See Robert M. Hutchins, *The Higher Learning in America* (New Haven: Yale University Press, 1936).

40. "Religion" is being used here not in the special sense employed by Barth and Bonhoeffer, i.e., as a form of human self-justification, or man's "upward reach for secure relation to some external or absolute reality," but rather as "those forms of conviction, belief, and behavior and those systems of thought in which men express their concerned responses to whatever they hold to be worthy of lasting and universal commitment," Clyde Holbrook's definition in *Religion, A Humanistic Field* (Englewood Cliffs, N.J.: Prentice-Hall, 1963), pp. 36-37.

41. Morison, *op. cit.*, p. 251.

42. Robert Michaelsen, "Religion in the Undergraduate Curriculum," in *The Making of Ministers*, eds. Keith R. Bridston and Dwight W. Culver (Minneapolis: Augsburg Publishing House, 1964), p. 45.

43. *Ibid.*, pp. 47-48. Cf. Hofstadter, *op. cit.*, pp. 183-185.

44. Of the nearly five hundred theological schools in existence today, more than half are unrelated to any larger educational enterprise, according to David Riesman and Christopher Jencks, "The Viability of the American College," in *The American College*, ed. Nevitt Sanford (New York: John Wiley & Sons, 1962), p. 81.

45. Michaelsen, *op. cit.*, p. 58. Cf. Robert Michaelsen, *The Scholarly Study of Religion in College and University* (New Haven: Society for Religion in Higher Education, 1964), and *The Study of Religion in American Universities* (New Haven: Society for Religion in Higher Educaton, 1965), as well as Holbrook's *Religion, A Humanistic Field*.

46. Hastings Rashdall, *The Universities of Europe in the Middle Ages* (2nd ed.; Oxford: The Clarendon Press, 1936), Vol. I, pp. 161 ff, 176-203.

47. W. H. Cowley, "The American System of Academic Government," found in Theodore Caplow and Reece J. McGee, *The Academic Marketplace* (New York: Basic Books, 1958), pp. 11-12.

48. Kerr, *op. cit.*, p. 21.

49. Metzger, *op. cit.*, pp. 8-9.

50. *Ibid.*, pp. 112-113.

51. Rudolph, *op. cit.*, pp. 136-155.

52. Kerr, *op. cit.*, pp. 21-22.

53. Metzger, *op. cit.*, p. 124. Cf. Robert M. MacIver, *Academic Freedom in Our Time* (New York: Columbia University Press, 1955).

54. *Bulletin*, American Association of University Professors, Vol. I (December 1915), p. 20.

55. Frederic Heimberger, "The Grass Roots of Campus Freedom," *Saturday Review*, Vol. XLVIII, No. 29 (July 17, 1965), p. 61.

56. Brother K. Basil, "In Loco Parentis: Somebodies or Nobodies?" *St. Mary's Dialogue* (1961), reprinted in *In Loco Parentis*, ed. Neal Johnson (Philadelphia: United States National Student Association, 1962). Mimeographed, p. 29.

57. See Harold Taylor's description of Sarah Lawrence College in the 1950's in "Freedom and Authority on the Campus," in *The American College*, pp. 774-810.

58. Throughout this study, the question of church colleges has been bracketed out, not because they have not become secularized in the three ways described above and are virtually indistinguishable in this sense from other institutions, but because by a variety of means, e.g., guaranteeing

denominational control of trustees, and maintenance of required religion courses and chapel worship, their parent bodies have protected them against this fourth aspect of secularization. Whether their denominational connections and overt religious practices alone distinguish church-controlled colleges from state and private schools and thereby justify their existence is a question constantly under discussion by Christian educators.

59. Hofstadter, op. cit., p. 114.

60. Ibid., p. 115.

61. Tewksbury, op. cit., p. 182.

62. Guy Snavely, The Church and the Four-Year College (New York: Harper & Bros., 1955), p. 137. Inadequate financial support, poor locations, overexpansion, and limited enrollments were also plaguing the church colleges, leading to the demise of many founded during this period, so that of the 500 colleges founded before 1860, scarcely 180 now survive (p. 8).

63. The best documentation of this era is to be found in Clarence P. Shedd, Two Centuries of Student Christian Movements: Their Origin and Intercollegiate Life (New York: Association Press, 1934).

64. Paul G. Kauper, "Law and Public Opinion," in Religion and the State University, ed. Erich A. Walter (Ann Arbor: University of Michigan Press, 1958), p. 78.

65. Samuel E. Morison, Harvard College in the Seventeenth Century (Cambridge: Harvard University Press, 1936), Vol. II, pp. 552-553.

66. Rudolph, op. cit., p. 170.

67. Earl McGrath, "The Control of Higher Education in America," Educational Record, Vol. XVII (April 1936), pp. 259-279.

68. Metzger, op. cit., p. 76.

Chapter 5

1. West, in Report on Consultation, op. cit., p. 18.

2. The term "church" is used here in the broadest sense, inclusive of churches or denominations, church boards or ecclesiastical structures, local churches or separate congregations, and individual Christians who identify themselves with Christ's ministry of humanization in the world. Since what is suggested here is not a program for institutional fulfillment in higher education but rather a prolegomenon to such programmatic thinking, no attempt has been made to direct what follows to denominational boards of Christian education, student Christian groups, or associations of campus chaplains.

3. Butler, God and the Secular Campus, pp. 28, 52.

4. John Dillenberger, "A Protestant Understanding of Church and University," in The Mission of the Christian College in the Modern World, report of the Third Quadrennial Convocation of Christian Colleges (Washington, D.C.: The Council of Protestant Colleges and Universities, 1962), p. 46.

5. Bernard A. Meland, "Religious Zeal: A Threat to Intellectual Life?" The Christian Scholar, Vol. XLI, No. 1 (March 1958), p. 48.

6. Michael Polanyi, "Faith and Reason," The Journal of Religion, Vol. XLI, No. 4 (October 1961), p. 244.

7. Harold E. Schilling, *On the Significance of Science for Religious Thought* (Nashville: Methodist Board of Education, 1964) (monograph), p. 2. Cf. Thomas S. Kuhn, *The Structure of Scientific Revolutions* (Chicago: University of Chicago Press, 1962), pp. 52-53, *et passim.*

8. Douglas Knight, "Religious Implications in the Humanities," in *Liberal Learning and Religion,* cd. Amos N. Wilder (New York: Harper & Bros., 1951), pp. 96-97.

9. Krister Stendahl, "Religion in the University," *The Church Review,* Vol. XXII, Nos. 2-3 (April-May 1964), p. 11.

10. Holbrook, *Religion, A Humanistic Field,* p. 39.

11. "Theology" is used here to denote "a specialized discipline involving systematic explication, articulation, and defense of a particular standpoint of faith," *ibid.,* p. 30.

12. E.g., the programs at Princeton University and the University of Pennsylvania. For an impressive statement of this case, see Arthur Magill, *The Place of Dogmatic Theology in the University* (Ph.D. dissertation, Yale University, 1960). Cf. *Theology and the University,* ed. John Coulson (Baltimore: Helicon Press; London: Darton, Longman & Todd, 1964), *passim.*

13. Charles Davis, "Theology and its Present Task," in *Theology and the University,* p. 114. Cf. Davis' article "Theology in Seminary Confinement," *The Downside Review,* No. 81 (October 1963), pp. 307-316.

14. *Reality,* p. 105.

15. *Ethics,* p. 103.

16. Robert McAfee Brown, "The Reformed Tradition and Higher Education," *The Christian Scholar,* Vol. XLI, No. 1 (March 1958), p. 35.

17. Since "autonomy" can mean either that a system is "totally self-contained and closed," or that the discipline has "a consistency of its own," it should be clear that the term is being used in the second, broader sense in reference to the disciplines of the university, since they can never be considered totally closed with respect to one another. Cf. Jean Ladriere, "Freedom of Research in the Physical Sciences," in *Truth and Freedom,* eds. Louis de Raeymaeker and others. (Duquesne Studies: Philosophical Series No. 5; Pittsburgh: Duquesne University Press, 1955), p. 93.

18. Malcolm McAfee, "The Role of the Expert in the Mission of the Parish," *The Christian Scholar,* Vol. XLV, No. 1 (Spring 1962), p. 33.

19. Nash, *The University and the Modern World,* p. 243.

20. Herberg, "Faith and Secular Learning," in *Christian Faith and Social Action,* p. 209. Cf. Cox, *The Secular City,* pp. 31-35.

21. Roger Mehl, in Report on Consultation, *op. cit.,* Appendix I, p. 6.

22. Dillenberger, "A Protestant Understanding of Church and University," *op. cit.,* p. 44.

23. Nash, *op. cit., passim.* Cf. Gustave Weigel's description of "naturalistic secularism" as the privileged theology of America in *The Modern God* (New York: The Macmillan Co., 1963), pp. 32-33.

24. Magill, *The Place of Dogmatic Theology in the University,* p. 32.

25. Miller, *Faith and Learning,* pp. 94-95.

26. J. Edward Dirks, "Diversity in the University," *Student World,* Vol. LV, No. 1 (1st Quarter 1962), pp. 65-66.

27. Flexner, *Universities: American, English, German*, p. 179.

28. J. Gordon Chamberlin, "Protestantism and Higher Education," lecture presented at the 18th Annual Meeting of the Board of Trustees of the United Christian Fellowship, Bowling Green State University, Bowling Green, Ohio, May 8, 1963. Mimeographed, p. 5.

29. Paul Goodman, "Thoughts on Berkeley," in *Revolution at Berkeley*, eds. Susan Gilmore and Michael V. Miller (New York: Dell Publishing Co., 1965), p. 27.